M000210932

Our stories seldom refle[...]
life can leave us wonder[...]
ten us or we just aren't a[...] [...] good plans. Ross
and Athena candidly share how God took two unlikely plots
and wove them together into a beautiful story of redemption.
If you need a dose of hope and a reminder that God works in
mysterious ways, grab this book! You'll surely be blessed!

Erica Wiggenhorn
International Bible teacher
Author of *An Unexpected Revival: Experiencing God's*
Goodness throughDisappointment and Doubt

If you're looking for a book that will strengthen your marriage,
reaffirm your mission, and clarify your purpose—as individuals and as a couple—this is it! Athena and Ross Holtz speak
honestly about their journey, including the challenges, the
opportunities, and the choices that have made this season of
their lives the best it can be. It's a love story, but it's also a
guidebook for those of us who want to finish well.

Carol and Gene Kent
Founders and directors of Speak Up Ministries
Authors of *Staying Power: Building a Stronger*
Marriage When Life Sends Its Worst

With raw honesty and practical wisdom, Ross and Athena share
how God adds his rescue, redemption, and restoration to weave
two individuals into a united "we" for his purpose and plan.

Pam Farrel
Author of fifty-eight books, including the bestselling
Men Are Like Waffles, Women Are Like Spaghetti

Together for a Purpose is a testament to God's faithfulness in
Ross and Athena Holtz's third chapter of life. Vulnerably and

honestly, they together lay out their struggles and commitment to work all things together for God's good purpose in their lives. I highly recommend it for new and seasoned couples who want to grow in their marriage relationship.

Janet Holm McHenry
Author of twenty-five books, including the bestselling *PrayerWalk*

The story of God's faithfulness in Ross and Athena's journey inspires hope and encouragement as two seasoned citizens come together for a new adventure. After the painful loss of a spouse for Ross and family and business for Athena, the challenges they face as well as the lessons they learn blend to create a bond that only God could provide.

Greg and Julie Gorman
Founders of MarriedForAPurpose.com

Ross and Athena have shared their hearts and bared their souls for the benefit of every married couple and those who are looking toward marriage. From the first chapter, through the incredible challenges they have faced together, and to the final chapter, they have allowed the reader to experience their challenges, tear-filled moments, and joy God has given them. This is not a book to just read . . . it is a study guide and God-given road map. Every married couple must read *Together for a Purpose*, and their lives will be richer and their marriage more fulfilling.

Chuck Stecker, PhD
Executive director of A Chosen Generation
Teaching pastor, Summit Church in Centennial, Colorado

WOW! *Together for a Purpose* is a wealth of hard-earned wisdom, wit, and the work required in relationships. It is beautifully written, relatable, and packs a powerful punch through life's lens. Ross and Athena's words are laced with love and commitment to each other and to the Messiah—the One who can bring marvelous from every mess and shows us His mission in marriage.

Tammy Whitehurst
Speaker, writer, and conference director

"The kingdom of God is made up of millions of stories that impact others" is my favorite takeaway from this beautiful book. This real-life romance account will give you hope, bring you joy, and show you how, even when life doesn't make sense, God is constantly working his good in the lives of couples who are called to His purpose.

Rhonda Stoppe
Speaker and best-selling author of *Real-Life Romance*

Ross and Athena are real, raw, and relatable. You'll find yourself nodding along as they tell the stories of how God came alongside them in heartache and hardship and how he met them in joy and new beginnings. They unpack life, marriage, work, and ministry with words of hard-earned wisdom and God's provision. If you're looking for a book to challenge you and encourage, you've found it. Ross and Athena share from the heart how God has been with them in the good days and the bad.

Mary R. Snyder
Speaker coach and podcast host of *Take the Stage*

TOGETHER

for a

PURPOSE

TOGETHER
for a
PURPOSE

LOVE AND MISSION IN MARRIAGE AND MINISTRY

Dr. Ross Holtz
Athena Dean Holtz

© 2022 by Dr. Ross Holtz and Athena Dean Holtz. All rights reserved.

Published by Redemption Press, PO Box 427, Enumclaw, WA 98022.
Toll-Free (844) 2REDEEM (273-3336)

Redemption Press is honored to present this title in partnership with the author. The views expressed or implied in this work are those of the author. Redemption Press provides our imprint seal representing design excellence, creative content, and high-quality production.

The author has tried to recreate events, locales, and conversations from memories of them. In order to maintain their anonymity, in some instances the names of individuals, some identifying characteristics, and some details may have been changed, such as physical properties, occupations, and places of residence.

Noncommercial interests may reproduce portions of this book without the express written permission of the author, provided the text does not exceed five hundred words. When reproducing text from this book, include the following credit line: "*Together for a Purpose* by Dr. Ross Holtz and Athena Dean Holtz. Used by permission."

Commercial interests: No part of this publication may be reproduced in any form, stored in a retrieval system, or transmitted in any form by any means—electronic, photocopy, recording, or otherwise—without prior written permission of the publisher/author, except as provided by United States of America copyright law.

All Scripture quotations, unless otherwise indicated, are taken from the Amplified® Bible, Copyright © 1954, 1958, 1987, by The Lockman Foundation. Used by permission. www.lockman.org.

Scripture quotations marked (CEV) are from the Contemporary English Version © 1991, 1992, 1995 by American Bible Society. Used by Permission.

Scripture quotations marked (CSB) are from the Christian Standard Bible®, Copyright © 2017 by Holman Bible Publishers. Used by permission. Christian Standard Bible® and CSB® are federally registered trademarks of Holman Bible Publishers.

Scripture quotations marked (ESV) are from The ESV® Bible (The Holy Bible, English Standard Version®), copyright © 2001 by Crossway, a publishing ministry of Good News Publishers. Used by permission. All rights reserved.

All Scripture quotations are from the (NASB®) New American Standard Bible®, Copyright © 1960, 1971, 1977, 1995, 2020 by The Lockman Foundation. Used by permission. All rights reserved. www.lockman.org.

Scripture quotations marked (NIV) are from the Holy Bible, New International Version®, NIV®. Copyright © 1973, 1978, 1984, 2011 by Biblica, Inc.™ Used by permission of Zondervan. All rights reserved worldwide. www.zondervan.com. The "NIV" and "New International Version" are trademarks registered in the United States Patent and Trademark Office by Biblica, Inc.™

Scripture quotations marked (NKJV) are from the New King James Version®. Copyright © 1982 by Thomas Nelson. Used by permission. All rights reserved.

Scripture quotations marked (NLT) are from the Holy Bible, New Living Translation, copyright ©1996, 2004, 2015 by Tyndale House Foundation. Used by permission of Tyndale House Publishers, Carol Stream, Illinois 60188. All rights reserved.

The Wycliffe Bible with Modern Spelling, copyright © 2001, 2010, 2011, 2012, 2013, 2015, Terry Noble.

ISBN 13: 978-1-951310-24-0 (Paperback)
978-1-951310-25-7 (Hardback)
978-1-951310-26-4 (ePub)

Library of Congress Catalog Card Number: 2022918810

Dedication

To the faithful God who brought us together, redeeming and restoring both of our lives—the One "who is able to do immeasurably more than all we ask or imagine, according to his power that is at work within us." (Eph. 3:20 NIV)

Foreword

Looking down I could feel my heart race as I sat in the chair across from Athena Dean Holtz.

My first writers conference
My first appointment.
My first conversation with the publisher.

I looked up not sure what to say and blurted out the words "I have no idea what I'm doing."

At that moment she spoke and immediately encouraged my soul. Her question prompted a conversation about my writing but more than that she brought hope to this frightened, new author!

Maybe, just maybe this writing thing is for me.

I had no idea that this brief encounter would change the trajectory of my life, for not only would I publish with her but she would become one of my dearest friends.

The first time I traveled alone to Washington to work for a week in Athena's home I was exposed to the beauty within the relationship she has with the one she calls her prince.

One evening after dinner at their favorite restaurant, Il Siciliano, they shared a piece of lemon mascarpone cake. During dessert Ross spoke to me of his beloved with such admiration and grace. He beamed as he articulated his version of the story that brought them together. His eyes twinkling as he recalled seeing her when she arrived in Enumclaw after being away for over a year. Even though she had spent time in his church before life took her to San Antonio, he spoke as if he was seeing her... really seeing her... for the very first time.

He knew... and dare I say, so did she... they would be together for the rest of their earthly forever.

That twinkle did not dissipate and continues today when they are together. The relationship they share brings encouragement to every marriage. As Ross says often, "It's not that they are perfect, but they are perfect for each other."

The twists and turns of life often lead us to places we dread to walk yet through it all Ross and Athena found a way to love again. You will find within their story God bringing together the most unlikely of people to finish well. Their journey recorded in this book will inspire you to do the same in your own relationship. You will come to recognize that you, too, are *Together for a Purpose.*

Within these pages you will find yourself laughing at their antics and crying in their struggle. Moments of tension will give you a glimpse of reality while tender occasions will make you smile. All the while you will be inspired to love your spouse well or perhaps realize in your loneliness that love can be found again.

Most of all, as you engage in their story, they will become like a friend and maybe... just maybe... your journey will lead to that little restaurant in the small town of Enumclaw sharing conversation with them over a piece of lemon mascarpone cake.

In the meantime, enjoy the adventure and embrace the passion Ross and Athena share as they inspire you to find love and mission in your own story!

Carol Tetzlaff
Author | Speaker | Bible Teacher
Ezra: Unleashing the Power of Praise

Acknowledgments

First and foremost, I thank Jesus every day for giving me this man to walk with through this final "trimester" of our lives. Without his direct leading and intervention, there wouldn't be a book to write.

Second, I am most grateful to my husband who had to sit before God and ask for inspiration to tell this story. I have to admit, he did the hard part, and I just came after and responded to whatever the Lord led him to share. And then Inger Logelin got to do the heavy lifting of rearranging and polishing and all the things gifted editors do to make a story shine. Thank you, Inger, for your dedication and the thirty-plus years of editing and friendship.

And last but not least, my team of friends and sisters in the Lord who have supported and encouraged me in my journey of leading Redemption Press and being a cheerleader for those with a message. You know who you are!

Ross says, "Amen."

Contents

And we know that in all things God works for the good of those who love him, who have been called according to his purpose. For those God foreknew he also predestined to be conformed to the image of his Son, that he might be the firstborn among many brothers and sisters. And those he predestined, he also called; those he called, he also justified; those he justified, he also glorified.

Romans 8:28–30 (NIV)

And we know that God causes everything to work together for the good of those who love God and are called according to his purpose for them. For God knew his people in advance, and he chose them to become like his Son, so that his Son would be the firstborn among many brothers and sisters. And having chosen them, he called them to come to him. And having called them, he gave them right standing with himself. And having given them right standing, he gave them his glory.

Romans 8:28–30 (NLT)

And we know that for those who love God all things work together for good, for those who are called according to his purpose. For those whom he foreknew he also predestined to be conformed to the image of his Son, in order that he might be the firstborn among many brothers. And those whom he predestined he also called, and those whom he called he also justified, and those whom he justified he also glorified.

Romans 8:28–30 (ESV)

Dear Reader,

This book is not meant to be a memoir. It does tell much of our story, but it is meant to be an encouraging word to those on the journey. We tell of our lives not to bring acclaim to ourselves but to tell of His goodness, grace, and patience with a couple of fellow pilgrims. We've included questions at the end of each chapter to promote discussion and to focus our points. We invite you along on our voyage of discovery as we seek to follow Jesus with purpose, passion, and joy.

Ross & Athena

Introduction

Margaret Atwood, in *Moral Disorder and Other Stories*,[1] wrote, "In the end, we'll all become stories." This is ours. Our purpose in writing this is not to bring some kind of glory or praise to ourselves. If we've written it correctly, it will bring honor and glory to the God whom we seek to serve with all our hearts.

This is a love story. It is not the story of two lovesick youngsters for whom the whole world is atwitter because of their attraction to one another. Nor is this a story of two people naive enough to think that all one needs is love or that physical love conquers all.

This is a story of two seasoned travelers who have gone through enough of life to know that without the love God has for us and gives us to offer others, love is a selfish enterprise that often leaves people unloved and unhappy.

It is a story of two Jesus followers who have learned the truth of Romans 8:28 (NLT) that tells us of a God who "causes everything to work together for the good of those who love God and are called according to his purpose for them." Patrick Rothfuss, a noted author of our time, wrote, "You have to be a bit of a liar to tell a story the right way."[2] I hope he is wrong. We've set out to tell the truth with all of life's twists and turns. We have attempted to show what God does to make all of our bad choices, mistakes, weaknesses, and even our sins into good— for us and for his kingdom.

Ah, but here's the thing. You, dear reader, are coming into the middle of the story. We have not yet reached the climax—we're still travelers and pilgrims. Only God himself knows how this story ends. We have chosen to each tell the story from our individual point of view so you get some insight into what we were thinking as well as what we did. We'd love to have you join us in the adventure.

Salman Rushdie wrote, "A book is a version of the world. If you do not like it, ignore it; or offer your own version in return."[3] But even if you like it, we want to encourage you to write your story. Tell the world what God has done for you.

—Ross Holtz

CHAPTER 1
When Worlds Collide

Ross

Are there discernible patterns in our lives? Are they given to us? Are they set in advance for us? Is there a "plan" for our lives that we must find if we are to have the life God intends for us?

I married Athena Dean in the sixty-eighth year of my life. I had been married for forty-nine years to my high school love. But nine months earlier my wife, Cathy, had made the transition from earth to Jesus's arms. I knew within a few months that the single life just was not for me. I wondered, *Who would want to marry a sixty-eight-year-old pastor with no retirement to speak of and a son and his family living in the same house?*

Well, through a series of unpredicted events, Athena and I found each other and married. Evidently, there was one person in the world who wanted to marry a sixty-eight-year-old pastor. The term "wedded bliss" aptly described us as we took a couple of weeks to travel around in my old motor home. We went to the West Coast in Washington, where we live, and then to the Cascade Mountains—getting to know each other and starting a new life together.

Athena had just restarted a publishing career that had been stolen from her a few years before, and I was pastoring a church that I had planted twenty-eight years before. We were excited to see what God had in store for us as a couple. We were both in good health, excited, and optimistic about the next chapter in our lives. We didn't expect it to be smooth water all the time, but we weren't at all prepared for the reality of what was to come.

The Summit, the small church in Enumclaw, Washington, that I pastored had been hit with a great deal of sadness—and change. Within less than a year after my wife died, a much-loved elder and an associate pastor both succumbed to cancer.

I had been focused on my own grief, and then the joy of finding Athena, and so hadn't totally understood the grief the congregation was going through. I thought they'd be glad that I hadn't been doomed to a single life. And many were ... but not all.

In the year after I married Athena, about one-third of the congregation left. It wasn't that they didn't like Athena. They did. But it was a change, and I guess they felt there had been too much change with the deaths, and they didn't choose to accept my remarriage.

There we were, a new business venture started, with all that entails, and a church in shock from the desertions. Our question of what God wanted from us took on a different feel entirely.

> Our dream world of wedded bliss was becoming something less blissful and more of a nightmare than a dream.

And there was my son, his wife, and two small, adorable but noisy children living in our home. I had invited them to come live with me after Cathy's death.

Nathan, my youngest son, suffered from bipolar disorder that had become so severe he was unable to work. We as a family hadn't yet come to the understanding that he couldn't work, only that he wouldn't. So there was tension and drama every day.

Our dream world of wedded bliss was becoming something less than blissful and more of a nightmare than a dream.

But we prevailed. The question was becoming less what God was doing but more what he was doing *with* us. It seemed obvious that he was at work, but were we up to the challenge? He had always been faithful.

But would *we* be?

Athena

I'll admit the tsunami waves our marriage caused in the church triggered me. My mom had always wanted me to be someone I wasn't, so the pain of that rejection was buried deep and, as of yet, unidentified and unhealed.

Maybe I was naive, but I hadn't a clue that a widowed pastor's remarriage could result in automatic disaster, often ending in a church split. I was aware that some of the older single women in the church were eyeing me with disapproval, and then they eventually left because I apparently got what they wanted.

> It was no longer me but *we*. And I was struggling to figure out how I fit.

My life had become chaotic on the outside, and I remained unaware of the chaos still inside me. The undealt-with trauma and continued fallout from my decade-plus of spiritual abuse and church hurt was still bubbling, and it erupted every time someone rejected me in one way or another.

For two years I had walked through my healing journey from all the deception and loss of my former life. I made my own decisions with little interference. I was learning who I was and growing in my identity in Christ. Now all of a sudden, everything had changed.

It was no longer me but *we*. And I was struggling to figure out how I fit.

What was God going to do with us—a sixty-one-year-old and a sixty-eight-year-old acting like a couple of teenagers, excited for our journey? We were so in love and happy at the thought of spending the rest of our days together.

Walking into our marriage with stars in my eyes, I didn't have any idea of the negative reactions heading toward us.

Discussion Questions
for Couples and Small Groups

1. What's your story? If they made a movie of your life, what would the title be?
2. Romans 8:28—what in your life has God turned to good that wasn't?
3. Can you name three unexpected events in your life that God put there to mature you?

CHAPTER 2

What's in a Name?

Ross

My name is Geoffrey Ross Holtz. That isn't the name I was given at birth. I was a small, redheaded, freckle-faced boy with a name I hated and couldn't pronounce correctly. Gaylord came out "Gaded," so my family called me Gade. The first day of school was always excruciating. In the fifties, when Red Skelton introduced a dufus character called Gaylord P. Sissy, I was mortified further.

When I was fifteen, the folk group I sang with, The Village Criers, was introduced by a San Jose disc jockey named Ross McGowen. Jabbing a thumb at me, he quipped, "I asked this next guy his name, and he said 'Gaylord.' I told him I asked for his name, not his sexual preference."

Ha-ha-ha-ha-ha. Jerk!

My efforts to go into show business waned significantly. Needing a regular paycheck, I went to work at Safeway. That was an okay job, but the hours were terrible. So I took a job as a sales rep for American Home Foods. I liked that job, but I hated introducing myself. Every time I stuck out my hand to a potential client, I just hated giving my name. Every time. It's really hard to be a salesman when no one knows your name.

But when I did use my name, no one seemed to understand it the first time, so I had to repeat it and sometimes spell it. No one could believe there really was a person named Gaylord.

I did learn to live with it, sort of. I had no idea, of course, how God would use all these horrible experiences to shape my life. I would even come to see some good in it.

When I got a job selling for Olivetti, I started using my middle name, which is Ross. I began signing documents G. Ross Holtz.

After the death of my late wife, I spent time taking inventory of my life. I had decided that finding a new wife was an absolute necessity for me. I thought, *What can I change to enhance my chances?* Believe me, I came up with a plethora of things that I'd change if I could. But my first name, the one given me that I'd always hated, seemed like a good—and relatively easy—place to start. But since everything legal, and my college degrees, were under G. Ross, I had to come up with something starting with G. I tried every name I could think of starting with my initial. Seems like I spent days until landing on Geoffrey. Geoffrey Ross Holtz. Yeah, that would work.

And it does.

By God's grace and direction, I was the third-born to parents already in their forties. There are some significant traits that most third-born or last-born share. I was both.

Dr. Kevin Leman, a psychologist who has studied birth order since 1967 and wrote *The Birth Order Book: Why You Are the Way You Are*,[4] describes me pretty accurately. He says youngest children in the family are typically charmers and manipulators. They love to get their own way, and they invariably do. Third-borns tend to be the most free-spirited due to their parents' increasingly laissez-faire attitude toward parenting the third time around. The baby of the family tends to have the following birth order traits: fun-loving, uncomplicated, manipulative, outgoing, attention-seeker, and self-centered. Hey, that's me, pretty much. I don't think I'm manipulative, Athena will comment, but the rest are me.

Dr. Leman further describes last-borns as generally not the strongest or the smartest in the room, so they develop their own ways of winning attention. He says they're natural charmers with outgoing and social personalities.

> I've always loved to be onstage, in the lights.

Dr. Leman finds it no surprise that many famous actors and comedians are the babies of their family or that they score higher in "agreeableness" on personality tests than firstborns.

But when he says that "the youngest often make a play for the spotlight" is when he most accurately explains me. I've always loved to be onstage, in the lights. When I played in a folk group as a teenager, I learned I had no problem with stage fright or excessive nervousness, a trait that has served me well as a preacher and public speaker. Fun-loving, uncomplicated, outgoing, attention-seeking, and self-centered. Though over the years I've tried to mediate these traits, even at seventy-five, these still describe me.

Athena

I have to admit, I hated my name too. Athena was not at all a common name, so nobody knew how to pronounce it. I got Athenia, Althena, Alta Dena, and Aretha. You name it, I got everything but Athena. I even tried changing my name to Tina so the horse show announcers wouldn't butcher my name, but Tina just never really caught on.

I was the epitome of a strong-willed child—bossy to the max and as talkative as the day was long. When my grandma was the guest of honor on the TV program *This Is Your Life* with Ralph Edwards, I stood next to the host, a determined five-year-old, pulling on his jacket as if to say, "Look at *me*!"

A few years later, I was sure Mrs. Gault, my third-grade teacher, hated me. I can't remember ever seeing her smile at me. She sent me to the hall with my desk for being too noisy, making other kids laugh, and always pushing to have the last word.

I loved to swim, and especially water ski, which I learned when I was all of four years old, along with any other type of activity where all eyes were on me. That grew into a love for

> I didn't know how to do anything small.

horses at age eleven after a week at Camp Hackensack in the Minnesota woods. This affection for horses would last almost a decade as I competed and won championships and ribbons and worked my way to my final show at Madison Square Garden. I didn't know how to do anything small. It's as if my motto was "go big or go home"!

I didn't have a very healthy family of origin, with an extremely critical mom who rarely said anything positive to me. She wanted me to stop being so noisy and strong-willed, to be more like my big brother—quiet, compliant, easy to mother and please. I was talkative, full of energy, and loved being the center of attention, much to her displeasure.

But my dad poured affirmation into me, saying, "You can do anything you want to do, if you just want to do it bad enough." He would support me in anything I wanted to excel in, and that was horses.

At every horse show and for every family holiday, he'd arrive on the scene with his bank of lights over his 8 mm movie camera. He put me on "the stage" and encouraged me to perform. With my competitive nature, I'd practice with my horse for hours to perfect my riding skills. My father affirmed me so much, I rarely second guessed myself and succeeded at anything I put my hand to.

> How would my outgoing and overachieving personality fit with Ross's?

My gregarious personality was naturally drawn to performing, not growing in knowledge and wisdom or critical-thinking skills. So, following in my natural-salesman dad's footsteps, I'd fly "by the seat of my pants" and go with the flow of any situation.

How would my outgoing and overachieving personality fit with Ross's? And how on earth would I fit in as the new wife of a much-loved pastor in a church that didn't seem to want me there?

Discussion Questions
for Couples and Small Groups

1. What "handicaps" did you start out with?
2. How has God used them?
3. Think about unmet expectations. We all have them. Talk about two that stand out in your life.

CHAPTER 3

Two = One

Ross

This is probably going to sound trite, but Athena fills my tank.

When my late wife died, I thought I was going to be alone for the duration. Oh, I have a large and loving family, but they have their own lives to live, and none of them want to cuddle on the couch with me. After the initial grief diminished, I was terribly lonely. One night, just to get out of the house, I went to a local pub for a beer and to watch football. At the bar were several "older" guys—regulars, one could tell—sitting there sipping their beer and pretending to watch the Seahawks. My immediate thought was, *Oh no, I don't want to be one of those guys!* I had to leave.

I prayed, "Oh, Lord, please don't let me become like that. Please, Father, I need a partner to spend the 'golden' years with. Please."

Just a few weeks later, I got a phone call from a missions group in Texas. This guy said, "Do you know Athena Dean?"

"I do. She used to attend my church."

He said, "She's moving back to Enumclaw, and we need a pastor to oversee her ministry there. Would you be willing to work with her?"

I didn't hesitate. "Why sure, I'd be delighted."

Some months before, I had read a post she'd published saying she would never come back to Enumclaw. It was a Friday afternoon; I can tell you exactly where I was standing. I thought to myself, *Athena is coming back to town. I wonder what that means? Hmmm, this could be interesting.*

A few weeks later, I was sitting in my car talking to Athena on the phone. I'd told her to give me a call sometime, since I had so much free time on my hands. She took me up on the offer, and as we talked, it seemed like she was kinda flirting with me. Yeah, really . . . go figure. I'm sixty-eight years old, and she's flirting with me? I'd not had a woman flirt with me in half a century. So I flirted back.

Of course, the way she tells the story, I started flirting first when I commented on something she liked as being on "my list." Either way, it was surprising.

> I'd not had a woman flirt with me in half a century.

At the end of the conversation, she mentioned that she'd be arriving at Sea-Tac Airport in a few days.

A light went on in my head. "Would you like me to pick you up?"

She paused, then replied, "That would be nice."

Wahoo! I said to myself. *Ha-ha, thank you, Jesus.*

A few days later, I was at Sea-Tac waiting for her. When she walked through the door, I knew, *I knew.* I knew that I was going to marry her. Just like that. She filled my heart. Like I said, trite or not, she fills my tank, my heart, my soul. She is God's gift to me.

So I say again, "Thank you, Jesus!"

I hadn't seen Athena in the couple of years since she had been a member of my congregation, although we had begun messaging each other when I agreed to be her accountability pastor for the ministry she was connected with in Texas.

The day of her arrival, I was excited and pleasantly nervous. Although this wasn't supposed to be a date, I thought about how I hadn't dated anyone but Cathy for over fifty years. But I was ready to start a new chapter in my life.

On the way to the airport, I planned the perfect first impressions. I had a new car and was wearing new clothes, but what about music? What kind of music should be playing in the car as we drove home?

Since I really didn't know her that well, I didn't know what she'd like to listen to. Rock 'n' roll? Folk? Classical? *What would be appropriately cool?* I wondered. I'm a child of the sixties, so "cool" is always important.

I was flipping through my musical library when I ran across Andrea Bocelli. *Ah yes*, that would do nicely. It would be appropriately highbrow without being boring. But what song? Then it came to me—"The Prayer" (with Celine Dion): "Lead us to a place, guide us with your grace." Oh, that really was the song of my heart; I hoped it would be hers.

It was, is, and that became our song.

The time from our first meeting at the airport to the day of our wedding turned out to be a little less than six months. We married in June. It was supposed to be in the fall, October or November, but summer was coming and we wanted to do some traveling and boating and such. Normal single people can get away with being alone for weeks on end, but Christians, especially Christian pastors, cannot.

I had a friend who'd been divorced before coming to Christ tell me, "It's easier to be single as an unbeliever. No one cares what you do."

So I asked my oldest son, who is the consigliere for the family, what he thought about us marrying earlier.

He said, "Go for it, Pop. The clan is totally behind you on what you choose to do."

So we sped things up and were married on June 13, 2014.

Not everyone accepted our plan. Apparently, there is some unwritten rule that pastors are supposed to wait five years or longer before remarrying. I looked in the Bible and couldn't find such a timetable.

I was sixty-seven years old when I started dating Athena. My father and my father-in-law both died at seventy-four. I didn't know if I had five years to wait. And since I didn't find any instruction from Scripture, we didn't wait five years.

I thought we'd have a small, quiet kind of wedding in my office with a couple of witnesses. But nooo, that's not the way it was going to be.

I said, "Athena, we can have a small, very small, intimate, oh-so-intimate, ceremony in my study. All we need is the marriage license and a couple of witnesses. I can get one of my pastor friends to officiate. Then we can go have Italian and a couple of glasses of wine, and we'll be off into wedded bliss."

"No." She didn't miss a beat. "That's not what I want."

"Wait, what? You want a church wedding?"

"I've never had a big church wedding, and that's what I want. With attendants and music and flowers and a dress."

I'm sure she was thinking, *Say yes to the dress*.

I don't remember much after that. I must have said, "Sure, why not? If it pleases you, it tickles me plumb to death." Or some fool thing, because when the fog lifted, we were shopping for rings. A couple of wedding bands should

> I'm sure she was thinking, *Say yes to the dress*.

have, in my very humble opinion, done the trick nicely. But no, once again I hadn't thought it through. I guess it makes sense that if one is going to have a fancy-schmancy dress-up church wedding, one must have a diamond engagement ring.

"Of course, darlin', we'll go see my friend Tom Poe, the jewelry guy. I do believe he'll have something that you'll like." Of course he would, and I knew it would be cheap too . . . *not*!

But we were having fun, and I really wanted her to get what she wanted. Yep, we were having fun.

After going through the experience of losing a lifetime partner, it's hard to imagine ever laughing again, let alone really having fun and making plans with a new partner. At first, I thought I'd want to be alone, but then I feared I *would* be. And then I wondered if I could ever love like that again. But by God's good grace, here we were livin', laughin', and makin' plans. I'd do

> By God's good grace, here we were livin', laughin', and makin' plans.

anything within my power to give her what she wanted.

It was a lavish affair to be sure—one to write home about. My first wedding was in the chapel of our church with just a few relatives and friends, so I started looking forward to this extravaganza. We had four attendants each. My oldest son, Bret, officiated. My daughter, Elizabeth, welcomed Athena into the Holtz clan with a Holtz Clan ring and a hug. And there was music—oh my yes, there was music. Garrett, Athena's oldest son, Bret, my oldest son, and Roger Peterson, who'd been my associate pastor for twenty-five years, played Rich Mullin's "Creed," the testimony of our commitments to Christ. Then Andy Newell and a friend sang "our song"—yes, "The Prayer."

It turned out to be everything she, and I too, wanted. There were close to five hundred people in attendance. Even some of the people who said they were going to leave the church, and did, came to see the show.

Then came the reception. We had plans to cut out early, you know; we had the motorhome all packed and ready to get out of town. That didn't happen. The reception, like the wedding, was a big event. Athena had people who planned and executed such events, and they spared no detail. Wine was "on the house." Fortunately, one of our friends, one who was very successful, stepped up to the open bar and told the bartenders to put the first $1,200 on his card. Thank you, Tim.

The music was provided by Roger and The Hubcaps, who billed themselves as the best rock 'n' roll band that never rehearses. The first part was true. They are the best at playing classic rock 'n' roll. But they do occasionally practice; that's easy to hear. Two of my sons play in the band—Bret on guitar and Thad on the bass. The Hubcaps played for hours and had several hundred people on the floor at all times. It was great, and we danced together late into the night. I think we were about the last to leave.

Yeah, it was that good.

Athena

After my first conversation with Ross on the phone while I was on my way back to Enumclaw from Texas, I *knew* this was it. I had earlier told God, "I don't want to date around. Lord, please bring '*the* guy' into my life so I'll know he's from you." I added, "I am not going to run after him, so he's going to have to make the first move."

So when Ross asked me to give him a call sometime, all sorts of fireworks went off in my heart. Then when he started casually asking me questions on that call, replying "check" after each one that was on his list, I just knew we were going to get married.

I thought about how his wife, Cathy, had pulled me aside only a few months after I'd started attending The Summit and said, "I told Ross if anything ever happened to me, he needs to marry you!" The way everything was coming together made it seem what Cathy had said was prophetic!

The weekend before I arrived back in Washington when Ross picked me up, I visited my firstborn son, Garrett, and his family in California. I spent time watching the TV program *Say Yes to the Dress* with my daughter-in-law and granddaughter. Seeing the excitement of the brides and the attendants as they shopped for "the dress" made me realize how much I'd missed.

At first, Garrett was a little alarmed at how quickly things were moving. "Mom, you're just now coming back from Texas— you don't even know this guy!"

I reminded him I had gone to his church for a year before heading out to San Antonio to help my brother care for our ninety-year-old mom with Alzheimer's. I knew he had been a faithful husband to his wife of forty-nine years, a family man, not flirty with other women. I knew he preached the truth and was very well respected in the community in which he'd served for nearly thirty years at that time.

As we began our relationship after Ross picked me up at the airport, it all came so naturally that we just both knew this was it. We learned more about each other and started daydreaming together about our future. Ross couldn't believe anyone would want to marry a sixty-eight-year-old pastor with no retirement savings, but I did!

He didn't get down on one knee to propose, but just a month after I arrived back in Washington, as he was dropping me off after an evening out for dinner, he looked in my eyes and asked, "Really, you would marry me?"

I smiled from one ear to the other and said, "Ross, there's no one I'd rather spend the rest of my life with."

From there, we starting ring shopping, and I picked out the most unique ring I'd ever seen . . . a lovely diamond surrounded by diamond chips with a wide band trimmed in more of those small twinkly gems.

Though I had been married before, I had never had a church wedding or a diamond engagement ring. I was nearly giddy with the idea of showing off what God had done. The redemption and restoration that God had worked was breathtaking, and I wanted everyone to know about the faithfulness of our God.

Finding the right dress was easier than I'd expected. I didn't want to spend hundreds of dollars on a dress I'd wear for one evening, so I was happy to find a long, cream-colored sheath dress with a lace bodice and pleated detachable train for $200! The open-toed, sling-backed shoes I found had matching lace. Rather than a complicated veil, I chose a simple cream silk headband edged with appliquéd silk flowers.

On a call with my firstborn, he continued to question me. "Come on, Mom, I don't have a problem with you getting married, but can it just be a normal guy? I mean, really, does it have to be to a *pastor*?"

> "Can it just be a normal guy? Does it really have to be a *pastor*?"

I guess I couldn't really blame him after my earlier poor choices when it came to whom I trusted in the ministry. I'd experienced more than just a few toxic and abusive pastors, so how did he know this wasn't just another one who would come in and divide and destroy my family?

"This man is different, Garrett," I assured my son. "He is trustworthy and kind. I've watched him pastor . . . he has good fruit in his ministry."

After my detour into deception earlier in life, the idea of having my son bring his hammered dulcimer and perform the song "Creed" at the wedding was important to me. I had been rescued from false doctrine and false teachings, and I wanted to declare the truth we were basing our union on. I was proud that Garrett had recorded the song with Third Day in the studio when they came into his area. Not only that, he almost won the part of Rich Mullins for the movie *Ragamuffin*, losing out because he wasn't strong on the piano, and that was required. I was still excited that he played all the hammered dulcimer scenes in the movie.

At one point in the ceremony, Ross and I faced each other and gazed into each other's eyes as "The Prayer" was performed.

I was in awe of the Lord allowing me the delight of finding love again after such heartbreak.

We didn't realize until the middle of the marriage ceremony that we'd forgotten the scarf to do the arm-binding ceremony. I'd never heard of this modified Celtic tradition that exemplifies singularity and unity in body and soul.

Nobody was alarmed; Ross just whispered to Bret, "I'll take off my tie and you can use that." He shook his head and started loosening his instead. We rolled with it and used the lavender tie to complete the symbolic act.

Looking back, I can see how that one response to a failure would set the stage for our marriage. We've learned to choose to look for solutions to the challenges we encounter as God leads us in his way.

Discussion Questions
for Couples and Small Groups

1. Talk about some situations in your life that God has redeemed, causing a major turnaround.
2. What has God done that has surprised you, for good or not so good?
3. How has your spouse surprised you—again, for good or not?

CHAPTER 4

The Exodus

Ross

When we announced our plan to marry, I thought, naively as it turned out, everyone who knew and loved me would be ecstatic. They weren't.

A guy that I had breakfast with almost every week drove into the church parking lot just as I was arriving one morning. He stomped up to me and said, "If you marry that woman, I don't think my wife and I can stay at the church."

I was shocked.

"Why would you do that? Is there a sin issue?"

"No, we just don't think it would be good for the church if you remarry, especially to her."

> I had never lived my life to please other people, only my Lord and Savior.

I knew that he and Athena had had a publishing issue that had, through no fault of Athena's, not gone well. But that was in the past, and as far as I knew, had been forgotten. I don't know if that was his motivation or not, but I had never lived my life to please other people, only my Lord and Savior. I had my family's blessing, and Cathy's too, and I felt I had God's blessing as well.

Stunned, I wasn't sure what to say. I asked, "Are you under the impression that I need your permission or approval to marry? If there was some sin to deal with, I could understand your interference, but I'm not seeking your approval or permission to marry Athena. You'll have to do what you feel is right."

Not that it matters much, but this gentleman was our top giver for several years in a row. I'm sure it mattered to him, as he and his wife disappeared.

My experience has been that when a person leaves a church, he or she feels an obligation to take others with them. This was no exception; they took several other families with them. People like to be with people who have money, even in the church.

A few days later, another good friend of this man called me on the phone. Now I have to tell you I have known this guy for a couple of decades. In fact, he had abandoned the church some years earlier—I don't know why—but a friend and I went to his home and lovingly cajoled him to come help us with men's ministry in our church. It took a little time, but he and his wife became major workers in The Summit.

This man and his wife summoned me to their home to talk about my upcoming marriage.

He said, "We have questions, and we'd like you to explain."

I really wanted to tell them to mind their own business, but they, too, were big supporters of our church, and we'd been friends a long time. So after church the next week, I accepted their invitation, or summons, and had dinner with them. They had lots of questions about Athena and wanted to know what was our hurry.

"Why not give it a few years and let's see how it develops?"

My response to them, and to others who suggested the same thing, was, "I'm sixty-eight years old. Statistically, I have a limited number of years left. We love each other and want to enjoy what years God gives us together."

Evidently, that wasn't a good answer, because that next week my friend called me and, obviously upset, said, "We want you to reconsider marrying now. If you don't, we don't see ourselves being able to stay at the church. How can I as your friend, stand by and watch you make what I consider to be a big mistake?"

"I appreciate your concern for my welfare, but we have very different views of a friend's responsibility to his friend. Warn me if you see danger, but if you think I'm going to be in trouble, shouldn't you stay close to help me up when I fall? Can't I disagree with you and still be your friend? Are we only friends if I do as you say? If I don't take your advice, I'm on my own, is that it? I'm not real sure we're talking about friendship here, much less Christian brotherhood."

> After we married, we lost about a third of our congregation.

After we married, we lost about a third of our congregation. I had no idea that this is not uncommon in churches. After the exodus, I discovered that people leaving a church in this situation was more the rule than the exception. Evidently, some people think that a pastor needs to wait five years or more before making such a move.

To be fair, there were other extenuating circumstances for the upheaval in the church.

Around the time of my engagement and wedding, Marianne, my associate pastor for women's ministries, died after a long bout with cancer. She had carved out an extremely successful ministry and was greatly appreciated and adored by the ladies of the church. It was obvious that there would be an impact; I just underestimated how much.

And a highly loved elder in our church also died of cancer. These were major changes in our little congregation, and people are often uncomfortable with change.

The axiom is: "When they grieve, they leave." It was part of the problem. For some of the people who left, I'd been instrumental in saving their marriages. I'd spent time in hospital rooms and emergency rooms with others of them. Hours and hours had been given on their behalf. "What have you done for me lately?" seemed be their thoughts and feelings. All I had done in service to them seemed to make little, if any, difference.

> "When they grieve, they leave."

I felt abandoned and betrayed by people I'd sacrificed for. What boggled my mind was I felt very strongly that Athena and I had a real purpose in our relationship.

Charlie Daniels, the country music giant, wrote a book called *Don't Look at the Empty Seats*. In it, he talked about the early days of his performing career. He spoke of the many, many nights he played to sparse audiences, where there were more empty seats than full ones. Athena and I had the privilege of speaking to him in Birmingham, Alabama, just a few years after he wrote the book.

> I spent many, many Sundays preaching to lots of empty seats.

After the exodus of the people who were unhappy with my remarriage, and because of the changes caused by the deaths,

I spent many, many Sundays preaching to lots of empty seats. I know of what Charlie Daniels spoke. It was hard to see the people who were there, because of the holes caused by so many empty chairs. Each one represented what I considered a failure on my part.

I have never regretted marrying Athena. What I regretted was that I was not a good enough pastor and leader to overcome this phenomenon. What had I not done, what had I not said that would have matured the people to a place that the changes of life wouldn't have thrown them a curveball? What had I taught that allowed them to think the church was all about them and what they liked?

> It feels to me like God has spent my whole life keeping me from getting too comfortable.

If there had been a sin issue, I could have repented, and maybe some would have come back. But somehow I had allowed these "sheep" to wander away from the fold because they felt uncomfortable.

Funny—well, not funny, but odd—it feels to me like God has spent my whole life keeping me from getting too comfortable.

In the kingdom, being comfortable often keeps people from growing or maturing. Have you ever seen an old man or woman settle into their favorite recliner? They make contented sighing noises as they relax their weary old bones into the chair. That's all well and good until they are required to get up and do something.

They say a body at rest longs to stay at rest. You've seen it. The person in the chair asks, "Can you get me a coke? Or a cup of coffee or a snack? Is there someone who will help me so I don't have to do to the work and become uncomfortable?"

That is the comfortable Christian. Don't ask him, or her, to change; it might make them uncomfortable, and that can't be the will of God, can it?

Sadly, I sometimes put more value on the people not there than the ones who were. I found myself wanting to preach, or scold maybe, those that weren't there rather than encourage and praise the ones that were.

> Sadly, I sometimes put more value on the people not there than the ones who were.

When I saw Mr. Daniels's book, I knew God was telling me something. Rather than lament those who had left, I should be grateful for those who'd stayed. Many later expressed that they were tempted to leave; they didn't really understand what all was going on. But they stayed, they supported us, and many still do.

One fellow who had a been a huge supporter of our ministry told me, "It's really hard now to come to this church 'cause all my friends have left."

I understand wanting to be with one's friends, but is that the basis of our commitment to a local fellowship—that's where my friends go? Not, that's where I can serve, or that's where I know God has called me, or that's where I'm a valued part, or that's where I can be the most help. No, that's where my friends are. Well, this guy and his wife stayed for a while but they eventually found a way to leave with a clear conscience, I guess.

Someone, probably in a book, once said, "Everything worth having is on the other side of our fear." It isn't in the Bible, but I think there is some truth to it. And one of the things people fear most is change and being uncomfortable. And I suspect I'm not that much different.

Do I sound bitter? Well, I struggled with that for a season. And I suspect that bitterness sneaks in every once in a while, but how do we find contentment with bitterness in our hearts?

I have discovered that much of it wasn't all about me either. People have to live with their idiosyncrasies and weaknesses, just as I do. So, for the most part, I've forgiven them, which for some is an ongoing process. I have learned not to focus on those not there but on the ones that are. And I have done a certain amount of teaching about experiencing the "uncomfortableness" of living like Jesus.

Who can I safely share these sinful and painful feelings and thoughts with? That's part of the deal with having a faithful believing wife who will point out my stinkin' thinkin'.

After losing more than a decade to a false prophet and a cult that he led, Athena has worked diligently to reestablish a Christian publishing house to serve the kingdom. We have been

> "Everything worth having is on the other side of our fear."

actively involved in ministries in the church and outside of it. It was my thought when we married that we would be "better together" in serving our Lord. It still is.

As I write this, almost nine years later, I tell you from deep in my heart and soul, I was right. My mother used to say, as I suppose so many moms used to say, "The proof is in the pudding." It was not a mistake for us to marry. We did have God's blessings, and we still do. We are excited and curious about what God has planned for us to do.

Athena

After Ross's wife, Cathy, died, my sweet husband-to-be wasn't aware of the women who were lining up to catch his eye. I learned that Cathy used to tell him about various women who had crushes on him, but he just never saw it. I don't think he was looking for it. He had been happily married for forty-nine years and did not have wandering eyes.

What confused me the most about the criticism we got was that no one really cared what Cathy wanted. She had made her wishes clear, not only to me and Ross but to their adult children. She had handpicked me to be the top of an actual list she made for the love of her life, but people were still mad.

The women in the church seemed to be the ones who were the most offended. The feeling was that Ross had replaced Cathy too quickly. It had been a little over five months after Cathy died when Ross and I began dating. I got the feeling that a suitable mourning period should be several years.

It was a hard lesson to learn that fallout was normal in a situation like this. Would we have waited longer if we'd known the congregation would implode? Hard to say. We just couldn't understand how anyone would not want their pastor to be happy.

I have to admit, as women began to give me the "stink eye" and act judgmental about our decision to marry, it definitely triggered the rejection from my past. I took it personally and assumed these people hated me and didn't find me worthy of their pastor.

One woman later told me, "Athena, I have to tell you that I struggled at first when you guys announced your intentions to marry. But as I talked it through with my hubby, I knew it was just my insecurities that were coming into play. It didn't have anything to do with you or the two of you as a couple. I realized that I was listening to the enemy's lie that if Ross could replace Cathy so quickly, then maybe my husband would do the same, and that really offended me!"

Seeing how relieved I was to hear this, she went on. "It went from caring about the other person's happiness to feeling my own anxieties and insecurities and focusing on those. How self-centered that was! Once I realized the root of those feelings, I repented and felt completely different. Where I thought we, too, would have to leave, I no longer felt that way. God had changed my heart, and I felt nothing but happiness about what God was doing in your relationship!"

> I assumed these people hated me and didn't find me worthy of their pastor.

This woman was one of the many who at first decided to leave until she saw the enemy's hand in the exodus and stood against it. While that gave me an understanding of what so many of the others were feeling, it still left a sting when I thought about it.

One evening as we sat around the dinner table at the home of one of the other elders, we heard a horror story about his mom and her new pastor-husband and how they'd survived as the church imploded over their remarriage. I hadn't realized it was normal for churches to be divided over the decision of a pastor to remarry.

At least that helped me process the pain and not take it so personally.

Nine years later, we have just completed a church merger. Both my husband and his new copastor, Marcus Kelly, have preached on how to see this union of two congregations that were blending to create something new and stay healthy. Marcus's words came with great wisdom and authority, as he has served as the chaplain for the Enumclaw Fire and Police departments for many years and has helped many families through their grief process.

Just before this, smoldering grief over my brother's suicide on Christmas Eve of 2021 had been stirred in me as I was doing a podcast interview with an author about grieving the sudden loss of a loved one. Then when Pastor Marcus delivered one of the most impactful sermons I've ever heard, I knew God was trying to get my attention.

Not only was I walking through the loss of my older brother, but the emotions of the merger compounded my grief. I really needed to hear what Marcus had to say about healthy grieving.

Sometimes the grief over my brother left me in an emotional fog and feeling numb. Other times I was angry that he not only left us without a will but with nine hangars filled with cars, motorcycles, bicycles, airplane parts, and a lot of junk. Every so often I would spiral down a dark tunnel of regret, feeling guilty about not having done more to engage with him, knowing well his struggle with depression over the years.

My sons and I went down to San Antonio to begin the clean-up of the mess left behind. Memories flooded me as we sorted through photos and packed up his apartment. When the feelings would come up, I tried to identify them and embrace them by being still, rather than running from them.

My normal drug of choice for pain is work, so I worked hard to *not* work during this time. But forty-five days after my loss, I had to dive into a very busy time as we produced our She Writes and Speaks Proclaim! Conference, our first in-person event since the COVID pandemic began two years earlier. When I could, I took moments of time to allow the feelings to wash over me rather than busy myself with work.

As I listened to Marcus's sermon on grief, I was reminded that it doesn't take a death for us to experience loss. It can be merely a change in the way things are done or the closing of a chapter in our lives or watching God close the door on a fifteen-year- or thirty-five-year work we've put our hand to and are now having to release. Change equals loss, and loss equals grief.

Pastor Marcus painted the picture of what grieving can feel like. It can be sadness, depression, bitterness, or frustration toward a situation that has changed. Frustration causes tension in our soul when we are grieving. Often, rather than identifying the grief and allowing space for us to process it with the Lord's help, we get offended at the change and simply walk away carrying that bitterness with us.

"If we just pull ourselves up by our bootstraps and don't connect with the loss and the grief, it turns into bitterness, and

> The grief was not identified, bitterness ruled the day, and people left.

we become numb and develop compassion fatigue," Marcus said. "That's where we are asked to meet a need as a volunteer or some other task at the church and we blow it off, no longer caring about those we've been asked to serve in the name of Christ."

Hearing this recently helped me look back at the exodus the church experienced and understand better what was really going on. The grief was not identified, bitterness ruled the day, and people left.

Identifying grief is sometimes tricky. If we find ourselves frustrated and snippy with our spouse, that's a pretty good sign we are struggling with change, grieving what we've lost or what we are in the process of losing. In order to live together with purpose, a great place to start is asking God to help us recognize our grief. And then we can process it together with our husband or wife.

Discussion Questions
for Couples and Small Groups

1. How have friends you depended on let you down? What have you learned?
2. Has your church family disappointed you? Betrayed you?
3. Charlie Daniels talks about not looking at the empty seats. Are there "empty seats" in the arena of your life? Are you focused on them? If you didn't focus on them, how would that change things?
4. Have you thought about the loss that change has brought about in your life? How did the grief express itself, and how did you process it?

CHAPTER 5

Ch-Ch-Changes

Ross

We both strongly feel we are together for a purpose. Defining that purpose and living it out is easier said than done but not as hard as some people told us it would be.

Marrying after the death of a spouse is an interesting thing. I knew enough not to compare the two women. And I knew there would be differences that I'd have to deal with, but some never even occurred to me.

Perhaps the biggest adjustment I've had to make is that for forty-nine years I was married to a stay-at-home wife and mom. Cathy had to work outside our home a few times, to help keep us afloat financially, but basically, she kept our home—by choice. She cooked, baked, organized, cleaned, and raised the kids. She washed and ironed my shirts and made sure there were groceries in the pantry. When family came over—one of her favorite times—she prepared the food and made sure everyone was comfortable and properly filled up and hydrated. The house was her domain, and everything outside the house was my responsibility.

Nearly everything rotated around my job, my schedule, and my obligations. When I made plans, I—of course—would check with Cathy to tell her of our plans, but seldom were there scheduling conflicts. Our vacations were planned around my time off, and even the time we ate dinner was usually planned around me.

Ah, then came the new wife . . . In many ways, Athena and Cathy were alike; they both were strong, opinionated people, and both highly intelligent. But in the domestic department, they couldn't have been more different. Some of the differences I knew, some I didn't.

> Ah, then came the new wife.

It has been fun being married to Athena and more than a little challenging. Oh, not challenging living with her, but challenging keeping up with her. She has more new ideas in a day than I have in a year. She's on the go from before the sun comes up until long after it's gone down. She always has some new thing in the works.

Athena works all over the country. She is not what I, or anyone who knows her, would call domesticated. When I say she works all over the country, I'm not exaggerating. She's gone many weeks during the year doing writers and speakers conferences. She lives with a computer in her lap and a phone in her hand.

> . . . not challenging living with her, but challenging keeping up with her.

In my previous life, my schedule and my routines were paramount. Not anymore. Before I make any plans, I now need to see how they affect her schedule. I have to ask if she's even going to be in the same town as I am.

Athena is in demand as a publisher, speaker, and teacher. You may not know, but all preachers want to be conference speakers. I'm no exception. I get invited, once in a great while, to speak or teach at a conference. I don't think I've ever turned one down. She, on the other hand, is constantly turning people down. She couldn't possibly accept them all—there aren't enough weeks, or weekends, in the year.

It is very hard on my ego. I know, I know, we don't like to talk about our egos, but everyone has one. And preachers— oh my soul, preachers have some of the biggest ones. I mean, who stands up in front of a couple of hundred people each week and says, "Y'all be quiet now. I'm gonna talk, and you need to listen to me. I have words from God." Who does that? Preachers. Every week.

When I hear her talking to some of the biggest names in the Christian publishing world, telling them, "I'm sorry, but I can't do that this year. Maybe next year," I want to say, "Hey, I'll do it. I know it's a women's conference, but I'll speak." I don't, but I want to.

> We all have our parts to play in the kingdom of God.

So off she goes with her team of creatives and marketers. As a matter of fact, as I'm writing this, I'm watching her pack to fly to Dallas to be on the faculty of Tammy Whitehurst's conference. I sometimes go to carry her bags and to meet her writer and speaker friends by the thousands. But I have a job and can't go most of the time. We all have our parts to play in the kingdom of God.

When we first started dating, I went with her to a Christian writers meeting. I was sitting with some guys I didn't know.

When she approached, this fellow who didn't know me said, "There is the Queen of Publishing."

I said, "Yes, I know, and I'm going to marry that queen."

Ha! He still probably doesn't know my name. Most of the people in her world don't remember my name. But they know her name—and now she bears mine! I win.

When Athena and I were dating, she lived in a kind of apartment over the Redemption Press offices. It had only the barest inkling of a kitchen, so we ate out all the time. The subject of cooking and baking never really floated to the top, as I remember. I was so happy to have female companionship again that the subject of ironed shirts never really came up either. She did tell me that work was her "drug of choice," but while we were dating, she was always available in the evenings for time with me. Many things I just assumed. And you know what they say about assuming.

After we got married, I learned that she *could* cook, a bit anyway, but she really wasn't drawn to it. This was okay for me; I truly enjoy eating out, which we did nearly every night. Fortunately for me, I've always like peanut butter sandwiches, and I've never been much for breakfast. She does have a talent for ordering in, I've discovered.

Nearly everything Athena does is in front of a computer. I learned that one could grocery shop from a laptop—imagine that!

I was taught to pick up after myself as a child, so housecleaning was not too much of a problem. I spent some time introducing Athena to a vacuum but, as it turns out, I must not be a very good teacher. Ha! With only the two of us living here, I don't have to vacuum too often.

The real issue was—*is*—time. Athena works all the time. Even when we are watching a movie on TV ... well ... *I'm* watching a movie on TV, she is on her phone checking and responding to email or conversing with someone about a book on her phone.

I look at her.

She looks back and nods. Says, "I'll only be a minute."

At first, I took her word for it. Yep, I'm sometimes a slow learner. We go out on the boat, and she always brings her laptop. One never knows

The real issue was—*is*—time.

when business will pop up. But I don't mind; she's happiest when she's busy.

The most difficult adjustment I've had to make is scheduling. Whereas I once ruled when it came to schedules, now everything I plan has to be run by her calendar, which is always full.

"Oh, we can't do that this week. I'll be in Nashville." Or Louisville. Or Dallas.

Or, "I'd love to, babe, but I'm doing a virtual conference that month." Or year. "But we can go maybe in 2030."

No, I exaggerate. But not much.

I have always taken my vacation in August because of the weather. And, because I've been at my job since before Noah built his boat, I get the month off. So, as usual, I'm making plans for time on the boat for my family and all that takes.

She says, "That will be fun. I'm in Dallas the first week and in Lexington the third week, but I have two days in between, and the fourth week is relatively clear. We can be on the boat then."

No, I'm *not* exaggerating.

That's the way our 2023 vacation plans are shaping up. I have a sabbatical coming the first three months of the year.

We're going to travel—Athena, me, and her computer, so she can keep up with the publishing business.

What can you expect when you marry the "Queen of Publishing"? Ahhh . . . but she's worth it.

Another area of minor conflict is in our religious practices. Oh, we are on the same page theologically. It's just that she is Charismatic and I'm Charismatic-lite. We sit together on the front row at church. When the music starts, she expects to stand, and she expects not to stand alone during worship.

> She is Charismatic and I'm Charismatic-lite.

If, perchance, I'm tired and want to sit down—I am, after all, going to be standing while preaching and she'll get to sit—I feel her leg against mine, and she whispers, "How can you sit during this song?"

As a Charismatic, she tolerates my Calvinism. She isn't trained enough to argue effectively with me, but I can feel at times her inner bewilderment. We agree on all the necessary theological areas, so we get along just fine, thank you.

Family, to me, is everything. Well . . . *almost* everything.

The Holtz clan is very close and tries to spend as much time together as we can. Athena's family, largely because of the spiritual abuse they all experienced, has been working to reestablish a closer relationship. I have to say she has worked very hard to overcome the damage the decade of deception did to her family. Bottom line, what Athena thought was a true church with honest motives to honor and serve God really was a con game—or more accurately, a cult. I don't mince words in my description of it.

Her first introduction to my clan was on Super Bowl Sunday 2014. The Seahawks were playing, and the family was all at my house to watch the game. I warned her that there would be shouting and yelling, as my family is passionate about the Seahawks.

I brought her to the door and reached for the knob. It swung wide open, and there was Thad, my second son, with green hair, a blue beard, and some kind of strange hat on his head. I laughed, as I was expecting something like this, but I'm sure she cringed and wondered what she'd gotten into.

But the day went great, and she got to see the clan in football mode. Oh, my family loves Athena and welcomed her into the clan. I know there were some inner struggles, but they all worked out.

Blending families is seldom easy. Because of the cult—which instructed her to cut off contact with her family, claiming they were infidels—it has taken some work for her to reconnect. At the time of our marriage, she had made apologies and reached out to her family. But they'd been hurt, and they were cautious.

> Both of us have been in enough spousal conflict to last a couple of lifetimes.

Then one of her sons said, "We're glad you are remarrying, but does it have to be to a preacher?"

They'd not had good experiences with their mom and preachers. But now I think they've learned to trust me and know that I'm not a cult leader. We've had fine times with them all. The hard part is they're spread all over the country, unlike mine, who all but one live within twenty minutes of my house. I think we have some work to do yet, but I'm confident that in the years to come we all will blend nicely. And we pray.

Athena and I have been able to resolve all conflicts with a minimum amount of collateral damage. As of writing this, we've yet to have a real fight. Did I mention that? Almost nine years and nothing that has caused raised voices or harsh words. Oh, we've had some disagreements and some rather emotional conversations, but nothing either of us would call a fight.

I have often wondered why this is. So far, I'm convinced it's because both of us have been in enough spousal conflict to last a couple of lifetimes. My first marriage lasted forty-nine years, but it certainly wasn't without conflict. Cathy and I were teenagers when we married, and we grew up together. Conflict was a part of that growing up experience. Athena had been abused by her former spouses and wounded by their betrayals. She never claims total innocence in the problems, but she was the one left wounded and scarred.

And then there is the age thing. I was sixty-eight when we married, and she was in her early sixties. What was there to fight about? We had a good income, so finances weren't a big thing. We didn't have children together, so there wasn't that to disagree over. The only thing that could cause dissention, but hasn't yet—not in a big way—was the business. Maybe there have just been too many miles behind each of us to waste time having a fight.

Ah, but I guess there is still time. Maybe after spending three months in a motorhome this next year, we'll not be able to say we've never had a fight.

But we'll pray.

Athena

In so many ways, we are opposites. Ross comes from a big, tight-knit family where the "clan" looks for any reason to gather. In contrast, each of us in my family of origin seemed to be an island unto itself. Big family get-togethers where siblings and daughters-in-law and grandkids all came together in unity were not a reality in my life. The closest I ever got was when we'd go and spend Christmas at my grandma Sue Sikking's house overlooking the Santa Monica beach. Those are sweet memories, so the chaos of the Holtz house, full of good-natured, fun-loving people, felt like home to me.

The Holtz family welcomed me and made me feel right at home, giving me an inside view of how siblings who love each other and are loyal to one another live . . . something I'd never seen in action before. It's the fruit of parents who made sibling loyalty and respect an expectation.

After some hurtful experiences in my family, and even in a church family, this was so healing for me. Watching family relationships weather the messiness of life and be strengthened is exhilarating and healing after growing up with parents who never really nurtured relationships at all.

But getting married late in life and blending two families was a tricky situation to navigate. Ross's adult kids still had to process the loss of their mom and deal with the grief that was overwhelming at times, even though their mom had told them he needed to get married quickly.

> Getting married late in life, and blending two families, was a tricky situation to navigate.

My adult kids, on the other hand, had some major trust issues and took a "wait and see" position.

Thanks to Cathy's preparation before she passed, we had a much easier time blending the two families than we otherwise would have.

Including both sides of the family in the process was important.

Ross wasn't looking for his kids' permission to remarry, just their support. I, on the other hand, was busy trying to sell my kids on the fact that I had found the real deal in Ross. We both wanted to make sure our decision to marry did not divide our family relationships.

The biggest hurdle was Ross's youngest son, Nathan, whose anger at God for taking his mom away made it difficult for him to rejoice with us as Ross's other three kids did. It took a few years before he finally began to call me "Momma," and that was a happy day in our house.

When we were first married, the chaos with Nathan and his wife and two kids living with us left me feeling like I didn't have a home. Because the two young children were noisy and unruly and our help or parenting advice wasn't welcome, they did their thing and we did ours. Ross and I kept to our routine of eating out, which was emotionally easier than trying to insert ourselves at mealtimes.

I was in my early sixties and hadn't been around little kids in, like, years. I'd come into a room and have to navigate over toys or find baby powder flung all over and spilled milk and cereal on the toddler table in the kitchen with two sticky chairs. I could either hide out in our bedroom or stay at the office, but most often I made my way out to the motorhome parked in the back of the house. My medication of choice when

> My medication of choice when the pain inside me triggered sorrow or anxiety was to bury myself in work.

the pain inside me triggered sorrow or anxiety was to bury myself in work.

I found out years later that the sense of friction and simmering anger was due to a misunderstanding between Ross and Nathan that he was not to remarry so he could focus his time on helping them save their broken relationship. Knowing my husband as I do, it's easy to imagine how he would have come across that way, especially early in his widowhood. My entering the picture triggered a feeling of betrayal in them, so it's no wonder I never felt welcomed by our "roommates" in the home.

As I shared this segment of the manuscript with Nathan's ex-wife, she shared more backstory and all that she was going through during those early days of our marriage. I had no clue the pain she was in with her life falling apart and regret I wasn't more sensitive to her at that time.

When I was single, I expressed my feelings, struggles, and victories freely in blogging and microblogging on social media. Now as a newlywed pastor's wife and a member of a shared household, I felt as if I were in a fishbowl. I couldn't process my feelings online because people reading could fill in the blanks and would no doubt try to figure out to whom I was referring. I actually started a pastor's wife's forum for a while to have a healthy space to process my struggles. Later I found a Facebook group of pastor's wives who shared their struggles, and no one was judged.

Another adjustment in our marriage was my first encounter with mental illness. Ross's youngest son, Nathan, had struggled almost his entire life with severe bipolar issues. I was often judgmental about how Ross navigated the problems that came up on a regular basis.

"If he doesn't do what you've asked, then there needs to be consequences!" I told Ross as if I were an expert on how to love and help someone struggling with bipolar. I spouted off more unhelpful suggestions to the point of pushing Ross away at times. It took a while, but I came to realize, along with Ross and others in the family, that we all had unrealistic expectations about what Nathan could manage on a daily basis.

By the time Nathan's marriage failed and the little family moved out after thirteen-and-a-half months (who's counting?), I had learned some lessons about extending grace to everyone involved and finding my own hiding place in God.

Ross is super easy to live with. He's very self-sufficient (unless I ask him to look for something in the fridge or a cabinet . . . then, well, not very). He does his own laundry, takes his shirts to the cleaners, makes a sandwich if he's hungry and I'm busy. In a word, he is very low-maintenance.

I had no idea how easy it would be to please this man while we were dating, but once we were married, I could see how perfectly God had given me just exactly what I need in a husband. He's someone who loves me well, a servant-leader who always reminds me, "I'm just perfect for you, you know!" He's strong but not controlling. He's confident in his manliness, so he isn't intimidated by my strengths. He is always there to bring me back to center if I seem to be going off the rails. He is patient and loyal and thoughtful.

> "I'm just perfect for you, you know."

Ross is also a one-woman man and super faithful. I don't have to worry about him cheating on me, which was such a kiss on the cheek from God. My first marriage was to a domestic abuser who was unfaithful many times during our short four-year marriage. Yes, God knew exactly what I needed, and he delivered—over and above all I could ever ask for or imagine!

When we married, I didn't really know what being a pastor's wife would be like. I had a business and a very busy schedule outside of church, but I wanted to be what Ross needed me to be. Sometimes it was just being a safe person for him to share with. I had to learn not to give him trite answers to his struggles or attempt to fix them but to just be safe and supportive. At times, my role as a helpmate was to plan getaways or prepare us to go out on the boat for a few days after the service on Sunday morning.

> I didn't really know what being a pastor's wife would be like.

It was a few years before I learned just how God-given our relationship was. I was blown away to find out that his dream job was to be a—wait for it—writer! He says he's had that dream since 2010. This guy wrote sermons every week but said his dream job was being a writer, and he ended up marrying me, a publisher! Who knew?

Early on in our marriage, Ross was named "Pastor of the Year" by the National Coalition of Ministry to Men (NCMM) for his outstanding work in men's ministries. I encouraged him to write a book about his experience with the conflict within so many churches between pastors and men's ministry leaders, and how God led him to support and encourage men's ministries. He and Chuck Stecker had brainstormed the idea a few years earlier. With the NCMM annual conference coming up, he got busy writing. *Are You in the Game or in the Way? A Question for Pastors and Men's Ministry Leaders* was birthed not long after my memoir, *Full Circle: Coming Home to the Faithfulness of God* came out in early 2017.

I guess part of the fact that we've never had a fight is that I avoid conflict at all costs. That avoidance has come back to bite me more than once.

My first husband broke my arm while I was nursing my six-month-old. Leading up to that, he broke my eardrum more than once as he pounded the side of my head when I made him angry driving in the car. Even though I didn't recognize God at that time in my life, he definitely delivered me from a very dangerous marriage.

Remarrying to a Vietnam vet with major PTSD while I was involved in Scientology and the New Age was an uphill challenge. I didn't even know what PTSD was, but he couldn't hold down a job for long, and his anger got triggered often, seemingly out of nowhere.

After we both got saved, we ended up together in the "Christian" cult. That eighteen-year marriage was destroyed by the false shepherd and his wife, who went on to emotionally and verbally abuse me for over a decade.

I wasn't raised around angry people, so when anger came to live in my house, I learned to avoid it. When someone raises their voice around me, my heart starts racing, and I go on high alert. All I want to do is disappear. I'm learning to recognize when I'm triggered and now can process and connect the dots as to why I'm feeling threatened. Ross has never yelled at me, but I've been around when others in the house are fighting, and I don't like it.

Part of the fallout from the cult is that I no longer see the glass half full but more often as half empty. If someone doesn't answer a text or email, I immediately assume the worst, thinking "She's mad at me," or "They don't like me anymore." There's still healing taking place from those years of spiritual abuse, but I'm learning more and more to recognize the lies I believed and take those thoughts captive.

Discussion Questions
for Couples and Small Groups

1. Do you feel a sense of purpose in your marriage? Can you articulate it?
2. Changes are sometimes fun, sometimes not so much. What changes have you successfully handled? What changes do you see on the horizon that you wonder about?
3. What about the changes in your spouse—are they easy to deal with, or have they become a detriment? How can you make it better?
4. At this stage of your life, are you enjoying it? Are there changes that God wants you or your spouse, or you two together, to make? Are you making them? Are you willing to make them? If no, why not?
5. How is your faith, or lack of, affecting the way you deal with changes?

CHAPTER 6

Greater than the Sum of Our Parts

Ross

Human beings are a unique species. When we are born there are certain attributes that come with our DNA. Our physical makeup is programmed into us. Some are gifted with a high intelligence; some are not. Some are naturally musical; some are not. Some are natural athletes, and some have trouble walking in a straight line. Anyway, you get the idea. Each of us is unique in some way.

And then there is personality. Everyone has a distinct personality; that is part of what makes us the person that we are. Hippocrates said there were four basic personality types: choleric, sanguine, melancholic, and phlegmatic. And, according to him, we all have a major type and an assortment of smatterings of some of the others. Again, it is unique to each of us.

Added to that, Romans 12 says when a person comes to faith in Jesus Christ, we are each given a spiritual gift or gifts. Every person is a complex, multifaceted, uniquely designed individual. Some of our attributes are good and helpful; some are troubling and difficult to overcome. We are, as they say, a mixture of "the good, the bad, and the ugly."

Then we get married and bring this mixed bag of who we are into the relationship. People have always asked me if I'm surprised at how many marriages end in divorce. I'm not. I'm surprised so many last as long as they do.

Take us for example. Athena is a strong choleric personality with a heavy dose of sanguine thrown in. Which means she is a dominant type A personality with a heavy dose of fun-loving cheerfulness added for good measure. The choleric part makes her a leader. Her sanguinity offsets

> She is a dominant, type-A personality with a heavy dose of fun-loving cheerfulness for good measure.

her dominance with an ability to laugh at herself and accept the criticism that often comes with her leadership. Her choleric part makes her a "get-things-done" kind of person, a visionary, an idea person. Her sanguine part often leads her merrily off in a new direction before the last project is totally accomplished. Complex? Why, yes, she is. She has areas in which she is impressively competent and areas that require "assistants."

Spiritually, she falls into the category of "prophet." That doesn't mean she can tell the future; it means she sees things more in black and white than in shades of gray. The prophet in her gives her a strong moral compass and heavy sense of right and wrong. I have to add, in love of course, this sometimes ends with a self-righteousness that is usually the burden of the prophetic gift.

> I am . . . easygoing, gentle, compatible, generally wishy-washy.

Then there is me, Ross. I am almost totally phlegmatic,

with a minor—really minor—choleric trait. The phlegmatic is easygoing, gentle, compatible, generally wishy-washy, as my late wife used to point out to me. Alfred E. Newman, of *Mad* magazine fame, described phlegmatics in his catchphrase, "What? Me worry?" I am not easily angered or reactionary. That would be a good thing except it's usually because I don't care enough about the issue. Things roll off my back because I don't tend to engage as fully as some people do.

Phlegmatics don't generally gravitate to leadership positions; we leave that to the cholerics when we can. But when forced, or led by God, into leadership, we are often competent because we are known to be levelheaded and compassionate.

Florence Littauer, in her work on temperament styles, said that one of the major downsides of dealing with the phlegmatic temperament is that they are usually hardheaded and stubborn. Yep, I can be that.

But I have the smattering of the choleric temperament, which comes to the rescue at times. I have been called by God to be a pastor, a job usually filled by cholerics, and have had to learn to listen to my minor tendency, which sometimes make me feel schizophrenic. I called Athena complex, but I must cop to the same characteristic. Which makes my point: bringing two people together in a marriage is highly problematic.

> My spiritual purpose is to help other people be what God has made them to be.

What makes it hard is that each person has her, or his, own point of view, history, preferences, strengths, weaknesses, and personality. Blending two individuals into "one flesh" requires compromise and submission one to another. For two strong-willed, opinionated people, that is never easy.

While Athena's primary spiritual gift is prophetic, mine is to be an encourager. My spiritual purpose is to help other people be what God has made them to be—to speak God's Word into people's lives and assist them in fulfilling God's purpose for them. With that comes the need to sometimes tell people they're going in the wrong direction—but to do it in such a way that they aren't stopped in their tracks and discouraged from progressing.

> We're not perfect, but we're perfect for each other.

And that is exactly what Athena needs. She, on the other hand, because of her gifting, has to sometime push me to "get off the dime" and reengage in the process at hand. Another advantage we have is that she and I have been around the block more than a few times. We have learned what works and what doesn't work in relationships. We are not perfect, but we're perfect for each other.

I've been in ministry for almost half a century. When I started out, we had compatibility tests for premarital counseling. Obviously, the point was to see if two people were compatible. I haven't seen one of these tests in several decades because what somebody discovered was that compatibility is more an issue of the will than of natural tendencies. At least that's my take on it. If people want to be compatible, they work at it and make it happen. Yeah, I know, that is simplistic, but hey, I'm phlegmatic.

Now Athena and I have an advantage many people don't have. I'm powerfully, I mean powerfully, attracted to strong, outspoken, clear-thinking, overly self-confident women. I was married to one for forty-nine years. When it came time to find a new partner, that was what I sought. And, surprise, surprise, I found one.

> I'm powerfully, I mean powerfully, attracted to strong, outspoken, clear-thinking, overly self-confident women.

Oh yes I did. By God's good grace, she was exactly what I was looking for.

And I, again by God's grace, am exactly what she needed. I am.

That's not self-aggrandizement; nine years together has proven it. I'm easygoing but stubborn. Athena can be an

> And I, by God's grace, am exactly what she needed.

"unstoppable force," but I can be, when necessary, an "immoveable object." But here's the kicker, as I've said before—we've not yet had our first fight. And it isn't because we haven't disagreed at times; it is because intuitively we know there is a purpose for our being together, and by God's grace of course.

We are greater than the sum of our parts. Our talents, abilities, personality traits, and spiritual giftings complement each other. Her tendency to take on big ideas with big challenges, and my saying, "Wait, there may be another way," work well together.

And her saying, "Ross, this project has to be finished," and my willingness to pay attention to her, often moves me on.

Solomon said, "Two people are better off than one, for they can help each other succeed. If one person falls, the other can reach out and help. But someone who falls alone is in real trouble" (Eccl. 4:9–10 NLT). Both of us know the truth in his statement. And, again by God's grace, we are committed to helping each other succeed in our given tasks and purposes.

We bring into our relationship all that we are, strong and weak, but together our strengths are expanded, and our weaknesses are mitigated. Better together—greater than the sum of our parts.

Athena

We are definitely opposites. I am a strong choleric personality, and Ross is the laid-back peacemaker, typical of a phlegmatic. He has always appreciated strong-willed women, but this is my first experience with a husband who is well suited for me. I think this gave us the foundation we needed to withstand the new challenges we met. God knew we each needed a spouse who would complement our strengths but, most importantly, each of our weaknesses. He was bringing together two senior adults, both with ministry mindsets and a commitment to building the kingdom of God. He had a plan, and we are learning just how intentional he was in bringing us together!

His strengths complete my weaknesses. My strengths complement his. His gentle way of approaching potentially volatile situations slows me down and helps me think things through. I want to act first and ask questions later. He asks questions to help me avoid costly mistakes.

Ross may see things through "Eeyore's eyes," especially on Mondays, the day most pastors want to throw in the towel. (Remember Winnie-the-Pooh's pessimistic and gloomy friend Eeyore in the A. A. Milne books?)

I had to really work hard at becoming a safe person to whom Ross could vent. At first when he'd say something like, "I just know it. Everyone is going to leave. We're going to have to close the doors. Maybe I should just throw in the towel!" I'd give him an unhelpful response, and I'd act all holier-than-thou and repeat back to him something he'd just preached.

"Oh, babe! Don't be an Eeyore! What do you think God is trying to teach you? Come on now . . . snap out of it."

You guessed it—that didn't go over well.

I am learning how to be a safe person to listen to both his disappointments and joys. Early on I tried to reason with him, fix his attitude, and remind him of what the Scriptures say. He's a bit of a pessimist, and I'm usually more optimistic, so I tend to have more hope than he does when someone has betrayed him or the storm seems especially fierce.

At first I'd tell him everything he was doing and thinking was wrong. But then I took up his offense when an older couple in the church told him, "Ross, you should just retire. You're all washed up. Let someone younger take over!" I found myself getting bitter as well and assuming the worst about many who even looked at me sideways. That was not at all helpful to my husband, so I had some major repenting to do.

> I am learning how to be a safe person to listen to both his disappointments and joys.

I will often encourage Ross in his preaching by sometimes going to both services. The input I gave from the Saturday night service would refine how he preached on Sunday morning.

Sometimes it's even, "Umm, that joke, babe, didn't work at all . . . I would ditch it!"

In return, there are times where he reads something I've posted or listened in on a meeting I've led and encourages me over the way I shepherd my team.

What a combo we are! Ross's phlegmatic personality keeps him ho-hum on many things that my prophetic (I like to call it exhortation) gift causes me to see as extremely important to address and resolve.

I'm the kind of person who expects repentance to include owning up to what's been done wrong, articulating what was done against me (or the person harmed), admitting the wrong, and asking for forgiveness. It doesn't work for me if someone just flippantly says, "If I've done anything that hurt your feelings, I'm sorry!" No, I want to hear them admit what they did! It also doesn't work for me when someone just excuses their bad behavior and blames it on being hungry, sick, or stressed out.

When someone creates hurt feelings and then just hopes it goes away, acting like nothing has happened the next time they see their victim, it really irks me—often to the point of not being willing to let it go because it is just so wrong!

This is where our differences can actually serve to temper the other. Sometimes I get Ross to take action when he doesn't really want to. But most often, his easygoing nature encourages me to be more forgiving, less judgmental . . . kind of like the Scripture says in Colossians 3:12–13 (ESV):

> Put on then, as God's chosen ones, holy and beloved,
> compassionate hearts, kindness, humility, meek-
> ness, and patience, bearing with one another and,
> if one has a complaint against another, forgiving

each other; as the Lord has forgiven you, so you also must forgive.

I entered this marriage after over a decade of spiritual abuse by people who micromanaged every part of my life in order to control what I said, thought, and did. Their aim was to protect and promote their own self-serving agenda. It is a breath of fresh air to have a life-partner who completes me, supports me, and loves me well, without an ulterior motive, other than to be the husband God created him to be for me! This serves to make me want to be the wife God created me to be for my prince.

> It is a breath of fresh air to have a life-partner who completes me and supports me and loves me well.

Is it always easy? No, of course not. But is it worth it for us both to be pliable and teachable as we see God working through our relationship? Absolutely, it is! Now have we disagreed on things? Oh, yes. Have I gone to bed with my feelings hurt now and again? Oh yes. He has learned to draw me out of myself and help me process my emotions. And I have learned to see the gift of his peacemaking skills as I grow in my new role.

Rather than seeing him as wrong because he doesn't respond like I do, I thank the Lord for giving me someone whose differences make me a better wife, mom, grandma, and boss.

Discussion Questions
for Couples and Small Groups

1. What do you honestly think about your uniqueness?
2. The personality differences between you and your spouse— are they celebrated or divisive?
3. Is Solomon's idea of two being stronger than one demonstrated in your marriage? How?
4. What baggage did you and your spouse bring into your marriage? Have you both handled it well?

CHAPTER 7

From Praying to Playing—
Strategies for Joy

Ross

We started our married life with high hopes, great confidence, and many challenges—some we knew would come, while some caught us off guard.

Early on, Athena and I began a prayer life together. I've always believed in the power of prayer, but I've never been very good at it. Oh, I know the mechanics of prayer, and I can lead people in communal prayers, but I have always struggled with being consistent in prayer—the "praying without ceasing" thing.

We agreed that the challenge of starting a marriage and a publishing company at the same time was a bit daunting. Well, daunting to me—she was full speed ahead. So we started praying together each morning as we headed out to our jobs and every evening as we ended our day.

Sometimes our prayers were simple and short: "Lead and guide us today, Father," and "Thanks for the blessings and challenges of this day" kind of prayers. As the needs of Redemption Press increased, our prayers became requests for His participation in our endeavors—having a need will do that to a person!

But as well as provision, we asked that he keep joy in our lives, together and as individuals. "Lord, teach us to receive your gifts of blessing and challenge with joyful hearts." We'd both been through some difficult times and discouraging times, but now the desire of our hearts was to experience the "joy of the Lord."

Chronologically, I'm a "seasoned" citizen. Over the years, I've learned to seize the moments that I'm blessed with. When I was young, I missed many of those small moments; I was always racing after something—a better job, more money,

> Rather than making occasions meaningful, we now take time to recognize they are already meaningful if we take time to enjoy them.

a better place to live, or some opportunity that was just outside my grasp. Now most of that racing is done. I don't seem to have it in me to chase anything quite that hard. Special moments are much sweeter to me now. Big occasions, like Christmas and birthdays, are still great, but a tender moment sharing a meal or enjoying a sunset has become too valuable to miss.

Rather than making occasions meaningful, we now take time to recognize they are already meaningful if we take time to enjoy them. And we are both getting pretty good at doing that, I think.

Both of us lead rather hectic lives and have heavy responsibilities in our respective jobs. It isn't easy for either of us to fully relax, as there is always something that needs to be done.

> A tender moment sharing a meal or enjoying a sunset have become too valuable to miss.

But, in a restaurant, those pressures slide into the background, even if it's only for a few hours. We savor those moments. It isn't that we're really foodies, although we both love to eat. It seems to be the atmosphere of a nice restaurant that we both find relaxing.

We are also able to relax on the boat, because it provides uninterrupted time. Well, relatively speaking. Athena always has a computer and her phone with her, and even I have been known to do a livestream or two from there. But, for the most part, we have time just to unwind and share quiet moments together.

We sometimes play dominoes, but usually we just talk—or don't talk. The gentle rocking of the boat has a calming effect on most people, and for the two of us it works as a tranquilizer. The water creates a boundary both physically and emotionally. It isn't that we can't be reached; it just makes it a bit harder. Most people, when they know we're on the water, tend to think of us as "away."

We listen to each other. In koine Greek, there are two words for listening. One is to simply hear what is said; the other is to hear with understanding. I think we work at that. Often there is more to the conversation than just the words spoken. There

> Often there is more to the conversation than just the words spoken.

is the tone of voice and the gestures or body language that accompany the words. Both of us have learned to ask questions.

In my opinion, to not "listen" is a form of disrespect, which is the other side of honoring.

As we ask questions, it often extends the conversation but yields a greater understanding. That is especially true when it comes to publishing. Athena knows everything there is to know about publishing. I don't. At times she'll have a conversation on the phone with me sitting alongside. She'll talk about things, sometimes problems, that I'm not aware of. When the phone call ends, I'll ask her about the comments. I can see in her eyes that she doesn't want to talk about it anymore.

Sometimes I'll say, "We'll talk about it when you want," and sometimes I'll ask more questions. Communication isn't too hard for us, but sometimes it isn't easy either.

Athena sometimes "shortcuts" her conversations. She assumes, sometimes wrongly, that I automatically understand her point without completely articulating it.

Often, I have to say, "Excuse me, I didn't totally get that."

It sometimes frustrates her, but usually she rephrases and explains it more fully. Her brain works faster than mine. She sometimes forgets I am not aware of the thousands of conversations she's had during the day.

We honor each other by compromising from time to time. She has interests and needs that aren't always convenient for me and vice versa. We don't "demand our own way" as the apostle Paul admonishes. Maybe it's because we are older, or maybe it's our personalities. And it isn't that we're hesitant to express our desires—we do—but we seek ways to accomplish the needs or desires the other has.

> We honor each other by compromising.

I am what's known as an "affirmation junkie." I can have ten people say positive things about a sermon or a talk, but if one negative comment is made, it eradicates the ten.

Athena is good about positive affirmations; they seem to come easy for her. I like that. Oh, it isn't that she won't disagree—she does—but she does it in as gentle a manner as she can. And I try to do the same. She gives me things she's written for my opinion. Mostly I agree with her. Sometimes I don't. I know she wants the truth. But she is sensitive to how I react.

I always want to encourage her, even if I disagree with her.

Athena

I haven't had to do a whole lot of sacrificing to have a joyful marriage. We just kind of melded together, even though the scope of my business is plenty different from his. I connect with groups and individuals online and through podcasts and conferences, while pretty much everyone in our small town knows my prince.

There isn't a lot of room for pride to reign when you're navigating a new marriage and family struggles that cannot be avoided. We fully embrace the truth that God is sovereign; he didn't miss these challenges coming; and if he didn't send them, he allowed them, so we can trust him with the outcome. As I acknowledge that God is on the throne and he doesn't miss a thing, it brings me peace that softens my heart.

I've also learned to do two things when conflict visits our marriage. First, talk it through with Ross. I tend to go silent and expect him to notice that I'm unhappy. I'm learning to verbally process to make sense of what's happening.

Second, I ask God in my own quiet times, "What is it you're trying to teach us in this?" I don't want to miss an opportunity to learn and grow. More often than not, I need to humble myself and recognize how self-righteous I'm being.

I also pray like David did when he said, "Keep me from lying to myself" in Psalm 119:29 (NLT).

Praying together in the morning helps us be in sync with each other as we start our day. Asking what we each have going on keeps us connected. And praying at the end of our day, when we are together, keeps those lines open. I don't do very well when I'm on the road in different time zones and sharing rooms with teammates, so I pray with those I'm with and text my updates and concerns to my honey.

> Praying together in the morning helps us be in sync with each other as we start our day.

Starting and ending each day praying together has done wonders for our ability to recognize and process our pain with each other. It's hard to stay upset with one another if we are going to commit the day to God or thank him for the day we've had. It's hard to fake authenticity.

I'll never forget the time I was not happy with a situation with one of the kids, and I hadn't really processed it with Ross.

"I don't want to pray with you right now! I'm too upset!" Hot tears began to roll down my cheeks.

I had to laugh at myself as I apologized for my behavior. And then we were ready to pray.

This daily practice to start and end our day before the throne of grace has helped us keep short accounts with forgiving hearts. This is a key to keeping our marriage joyful!

When I travel or am busy at the office, Ross is always good at texting to touch base and see how I'm doing, keeping me up to speed on things happening at home with family issues or at the church. A FaceTime here or there fills in the gaps.

Whether it's a birthday or anniversary or celebrating the birthday of Redemption Press, we decide on a place to go and enjoy reminiscing about our life together. Sometimes it's Holtz clan stories, especially boating trips and other escapades. We often rehearse the stories of our lives and find it meaningful to connect the dots to highlight what God has done.

The annual three-generation birthday on March 4 celebrating Ross, Nathan, and Christian—his firstborn grandson—is sometimes a day of bowling, a dinner out, or a party at the house. Seahawks games are normally enjoyed as a family in our living room with much raucous celebration.

Memorial Day and Labor Day weekends have many times been spent east of the mountains at Ross's second-born's place. The Holtz clan brings their trailers, tents, and motorhomes and spends the days on the Columbia River with tubes and wakeboards for the kids and evenings around the fire strumming and singing.

Then Thanksgiving and Christmas are always spent around our dining room table with as many of the family as are around and available. We have traditions on what is served— usually turkey or prime rib roasted on the Traeger grill (the one thing Ross knows how to cook on and is totally responsible for!) and a Norwegian salad provided by one of the daughters-in law.

We love to go out on the water in our forty-plus-year-old sailboat. Even if we don't take it out of the slip, or simply go around the corner from the marina onto the long dock, being on the water is soothing and rejuvenates us. We realized early on that taking off after the Sunday service until Tuesday morning felt to us like taking a whole week off.

I especially like a spot at the Foss Waterway just underneath the Foss Waterway Maritime Museum where many times a barge is waiting to take off. When it does, there's all sorts of rocking and rolling from the propellers on the tugs pulling them out into open waters. The gentle movement while docked on the long dock takes me back to my times as a young girl on my dad's boat, gently rocking in the breeze.

Being on the water in our boat, looking at the reflections of boats and lights, and watching the sunsets, restores my weary soul. I love watching for spiritual parallels in God's beauty in my surroundings and sharing them with others.

> Being on the water . . . restores my weary soul.

We find joy in scoping out new scenic destinations in our motorhome for a couple of days—not hard to find in the Pacific Northwest. We can go twenty minutes away to a lake or two hours away up to La Conner in the Skagit Valley, where we stay in the marina RV park. Either is always fun for me. We both love the little town and have our favorite restaurants and views of the water. I find it refreshing to walk along the dock by the Swinomish Channel, look at boats and clouds, and enjoy the sunset. Getting away like that is pretty simple and not expensive but rejuvenating. Sometimes we will go during

April and enjoy the color and beauty of the annual tulip festival along the way.

One day, the sun was shining after church, and Mount Rainier was "out," as we say in the Northwest. So we hopped into my aqua Mini Cooper convertible and made a Sunday afternoon of driving completely around the forest roads at the base of Mt. Rainier. It was absolutely exhilarating, and all it took was a tank of gas and an appreciation of God's magnificent creation!

When it comes to our "love languages," we both enjoy physical touch and words of affirmation, so this is an easy one for us. I often reach over to hold Ross's hand or tell him, "Did I ever tell you how much I love you?" or "I'm so glad God gave you to me."

We often have the fireplace going in the living room when it's cold or damp out and snuggle next to one another on the couch watching British murder mysteries. We are both avid readers, so often we just read silently without feeling the need to talk—just being together is comforting. We do both appreciate gifts and quality time as part of our "love languages," but we can easily sit by one another reading, without saying a word. Neither one of us feels the need to fill up blank air with words.

Ross always wants to find out what I want to do, and if he is able, he says, "It tickles me plumb to death to do whatever meets your fancy."

I always feel heard and loved by him.

Both of us do love trying new restaurants and going to our all-time favorite, Il Siciliano in Enumclaw. Whether tasting a new dish or one we've enjoyed before, I'm happy just sitting across the table from my guy and counting my blessings. My list of blessings always ends with my biggest gift.

I tell Ross frequently, "I'm sure glad you married me!"

He's a man who loves me well, balances me out, and shows me what "emotionally healthy" looks like in a marriage. Sometimes I get weepy as I think of how grateful I am for this man!

Discussion Questions
for Couples and Small Groups

1. How would you rate your prayer life? Good, fair, improving, nonexistent?

2. How have the years seasoned you? Are you aging like fine wine or like milk?

3. What do you and your spouse do to enhance your time together?

4. Are you a listener? Do you hear with understanding or passively listen?

CHAPTER 8

What Am I Here For?

Ross

"What am I here for? What's my purpose?"

Have you ever asked that? You probably have. My guess would be that people have been asking that since the beginning, or close to it anyway.

A couple of weeks ago, a man said to me, "I have no purpose for living, no reason to be alive." A week later, this same man saved a kid's life after an overdose of fentanyl by applying CPR.

When I spoke to him next, I told him, "If that's all you ever did in your whole life, your life had meaning."

What are we here for? Is there a purpose for our life? Merriam-Webster.com defines purpose as, "Something set up as an object or end to be attained: intention, an anticipated outcome that is intended or that guides planned actions; something that we planned for, worked for, hoped for."

Our purpose helps us to plan our actions. Pretty important part of our intentional life, don't you think? Purpose is sometimes called "our mission."

Is it important for us to know our purpose, our mission? I read an article a while ago that said when we have a sense of purpose, we tend to have increased optimism, resiliency, and hope. We then experience joy, happiness, and satisfaction more often. Wow, isn't that what most people are seeking—joy, happiness, and satisfaction?

The Bible says that God has shaped and prepared us to play a unique role in each step of our story and in the lives of others. It says, "For we are his workmanship, created in Christ Jesus for good works, which God prepared beforehand, that we should walk in them" (Eph. 2:10 ESV). It also says, "And we know that for those who love God all things work together for good, for those who are called according to his purpose" (Rom. 8:28 ESV). So it isn't only our purpose but his. That makes it doubly important to know that purpose.

But it's not enough to know the purpose. We are to live it. First Corinthians 7:17 (ESV) says, "Only let each person lead the life that the Lord has assigned to him, and to which God has called him." The life assigned to us by God.

How much control God exercises over each of our lives has been argued for a millennium. The Bible says God is sovereign, but it also says he gives us choices to be made. There is a life assigned to us—that's what it says. A certain amount of that is beyond our choices; where we were born, to whom we were born, and the DNA we were given. In all these we were given no choice. But how we live certainly depends on choices God gives us to make. Do we follow him? Are we obedient to his instructions? We do have choices in these.

> How we live depends on choices that God gives us to make.

This reality doesn't only apply to us as individuals but to us as married couples or part of a family structure. We don't live to ourselves only, do we? What we do has consequences not only for ourselves but for those with whom we have a relationship.

So I'm thinking, what has God assigned to Athena and me? We both completely believe God put us together, or certainly approved of our choice, however you look at it. So now the question has to be asked, what does he want for us—what is our purpose together?

Where do we start? We have to consider all those attributes that we've already discussed: our gifts, talents, abilities, what we've learned from the years we've lived, and what opportunities God has afforded us. Quite a list indeed.

When I married Athena, I'd been in vocational ministry for over forty years. Pastoring is my calling; it is where God led me from a very early age. I've been trained and educated in my vocation. It is now who I am and what I'm about.

> Our marriage started a new chapter in our lives, but the old has not passed away.

Admittedly, our marriage started a new chapter in our lives—and God speaks often about doing a new thing—but the old has not passed away. I am still a pastor at heart and by experience and training.

Athena, on the other hand, came to faith as an adult. Her background was in business. She came with years of experience in that field. She'd even published books about her experiences there. By her own words, she started ministry as a novice to Christianity, something the Bible warns against. She and her then husband, Chuck, started a Christian publishing house called WinePress. It was very successful until she, being inexperienced in her faith, fell under the leadership of a spiritual fraud, who ended up owning her business and left her virtually on the streets—well, couch surfing. She survived and became a radio personality.

Then, just as we were starting our relationship, she was called back into the publishing business, starting Redemption Press.

Coming together, we brought our experiences, our successes, our failures, our scars, our hopes, and our dreams into what the Bible would call

> What we needed was an email from God outlining our next moves.

a new thing. Now what were we going to do with all of that? A new chapter indeed. What we needed was an email from God outlining our next moves. Not getting that, and knowing his grace is sufficient, we prayed and prayed and made the choice in faith as best we could. Grace and prayer—what an unbeatable combination.

Starting a business, even one called a Christian business, is not easy. We knew God had a plan, but his having a plan doesn't necessarily mean it is an easy path.

For the first eight years of our marriage, Athena ran Redemption Press with occasional input from me, and I served as the senior pastor of the church I planted thirty-six years ago. The business had ups and downs as all startups have. But it survived and is thriving. My ministry, because of my advanced age, has come to a transitional time. Her dream of once again being in Christian publishing was developing; my years as a senior pastor were winding down.

All along the way of our marriage and in the development of Redemption Press, we prayed. We prayed to know God's will in every situation and circumstance that developed. We made mistakes. Surely that doesn't surprise

> We continually asked, "Lord, what is your plan, what is your purpose for us?"

you. At times we missed his instructions and had to retrace our steps. And we continually asked, "Lord, what is your plan? What is your purpose—for each of us and for the business and for our ministries individually and together?" My guess is we'll be doing that for the duration.

In Lewis Carroll's *Alice in Wonderland*, there is an exceptionally insightful discussion between Alice and the Cheshire Cat:

> Alice: "Would you tell me, please, which way I ought to go from here?"
> The Cheshire Cat: "That depends a good deal on where you want to get to."
> Alice: "I don't much care where."
> The Cheshire Cat: "Then it doesn't much matter which way you go."
> Alice: "So long as I get somewhere."
> The Cheshire Cat: "Oh, you're sure to do that, if only you walk long enough."

We knew where we wanted to go. But where did God want us to go? He has a purpose, and by faith we were determined to find his purpose and make it ours. We've both found that asking him to make our purpose his didn't work sufficiently well. Scriptures tell us, "We can make our plans, but the Lord determines our steps" (Prov. 16:9 NLT).

What we did know: God is sovereign. We knew that we wanted to honor and glorify him in all we did. And we knew our strengths and our weaknesses. So we started there.

Athena

When bad things happen, have you heard Christians assure each other, "Don't worry, it'll all work out for the best!" And then they often quote part of Romans 8:28 about God working "all things together for good."

After my disastrous experience in the controlling religious cult, I never want to be accused of cherry-picking Scriptures and quoting them out of context. Been there, done that, and had it drummed into me by expert "cherry-pickers."

The first part of Romans 8:28 says, "And we know that God works all things together for good . . ." But is that promise for all?

No. It's only for those who love God and are called according to his purposes (the second part of that verse).

Yes, it's good news that our God works *all things* together for good (yes, even the bad things) for those who love him and are called according to his purposes. But wait—there is more to it!

The next verse brings us back to the purpose of Romans 8:28, the purpose of God working "all things together for good," which is Romans 8:29. And it is usually not included when Romans 8:28 is mentioned. The first part of verse 29 (ESV) says: "For those whom he foreknew he also predestined to be conformed to the image of his Son."

I believe our God brings good out of some very bad circumstances and experiences *so* we might be conformed to the image of Jesus.

Those hard times of suffering, loss, grief, and abuse are opportunities for us to be conformed to the image of Christ. God uses suffering to strengthen and deepen our roots and cause us to cling to our Savior as we process our pain.

I will never forget how God drew me into deeper intimacy with himself as he redeemed what was stolen from me, primarily my voice. The end of my detour into deception found me completely silenced. My twenty-year-old publishing platform was pulled out from under me, my company stolen. I was not allowed to speak to the authors I'd brought into WinePress or even other employees. I'd been branded the rebellious one and told they could not trust what might come out of my mouth.

> Those hard times of suffering, loss, grief, and abuse are opportunities for us to be conformed to the image of Christ.

That attempt by the enemy to muzzle and fully mute me was excruciating. However, to keep my entire belief system at the time from crumbling, I had to keep telling myself *This is God's discipline for me.* I kept quoting Hebrews 12:11 to myself: "No discipline seems pleasant at the time, but painful. Later on, however, it produces a harvest of righteousness and peace for those who have been trained by it" (NIV). I told myself, *I must learn from this!*

It wasn't long before God opened my eyes and released me from the prison of deception. As he began to heal me and restore me, he gave me back my voice through a radio show I named *Always Faithful*. He had proven himself to me and redeemed and restored much of what had been stolen, but I was only halfway back to God's plan to restore what the locusts had eaten.

My voice had been completely silenced, and WinePress was taken out of my hands in 2010. In late 2011, I walked away, heartbroken, from the company I had cofounded twenty years earlier.

A full decade later, in 2021, I was honored with the Best Female Podcaster Award by the nationwide Spark Media for my podcast, *All Things*, based on Romans 8:28. Our faithful God had redeemed my voice—and my ability to communicate his truth after all the loss I'd experienced!

> Our faithful God has redeemed my voice . . . after all the loss I'd experienced.

Romans 8:28 became my go-to verse to praise God for redeeming and restoring my life after all the destruction I'd experienced. And I will stand on this truth that he will never waste our pain and will always bring good out of whatever he allows to come into our lives, no matter how devastating.

But over the past few years, my focus has shifted to also include the *reason* God brings good out of all things. It's not just to have everything turn out the way we want. God has a goal in this process! He is at work conforming us to the likeness of Christ.

Romans 8:29 in the *Amplified Bible* puts it this way: "For those whom He foreknew [of whom He was aware and loved beforehand], He also destined from the beginning [foreordaining them] to be molded into the image of His Son [and share inwardly His likeness]."

The *New Living Translation* says: "He chose them to become like his Son."

The Wycliffe Bible with Modern Spelling says, "By grace to be made like to the image of his Son . . ."

The word "conform" means "to make similar in form, nature or character" (dictionary.com). Oh how I long to be more like him . . . that my character would be like Christ's. And oh, how far I have to go. But that's where my focus is . . . not only on all God has done to bring good out of the struggles in our lives but also to make the two of us, as a couple, more like himself.

Living together with a purpose with all of our baggage and expectations and assumptions and fears takes gratitude, humility, and a teachable spirit. I find myself in hard situations not just looking for the good but asking God, "What can I learn here that will conform me to the image of your Son?"

Discussion Questions
for Couples and Small Groups

1. What are you here for? Can you articulate what your purpose is? What has God called you to do?
2. How about your marriage—does it have a purpose? Can you define it?
3. Has your purpose changed with the "seasoning" of time and age? How so?

CHAPTER 9

People and Purpose

Ross

My job pastoring a church I'd planted more than thirty years before could be done almost by rote. The challenges and needs were largely expected and anticipated. But Redemption Press was, as they say, a horse of a different color.

Athena knew the publishing business inside and out, having started a successful publishing house before. But times were different now, and there was competition that she'd not had previously. This was going to require a new level of prayer for both of us—for her to be the leader and business person she needed to be, and for me to learn to be supporting staff rather than the boss. This was going to require a great deal of prayer for guidance and provision.

> The first real challenge was in managing personnel.

There were any number of challenges starting out, but the first real challenge was in managing personnel. Bringing in people who had no experience in publishing, and some who didn't even have good tech or computer skills, was definitely a challenge.

Athena even tried bringing on her youngest son, hoping to help try to repair their relationship. It only did more damage because, as a visionary, she struggled with communicating with her son. We found out many years later that those who had gone through the process of publishing with Redemption Press themselves seemed to make some of the best team members.

There were some major changes in personnel as we got things going, but I advised Athena as best I could, and we prayed about it. And the company charged ahead. Well, maybe not charged, but at least it was moving in the right direction.

Athena was heartbroken and more than a little discouraged every time those she hired didn't prove to be a good fit in the company. But with her choleric persuasion, she picked herself up and took on the next challenge and conflict.

And we prayed, "Lord, give us compassion for people we disagree with and a heart to love those who don't love us. And we need authors to publish." Our prayer can't always be on the spiritual side; sometimes we just need God to provide for our physical needs. Know what I mean?

Redemption Press has a motto: "Your Message—Our Mission." I like that. I have a doctor of ministry and a doctor of divinity degree. I've been in ministry for nearly half a century. I know something about speaking God's Word. I know about preaching. I knew nothing about the ministry of writing.

I know some authors, most of whom are seminary professors or pastors of huge churches. But what of Betty Jane who has written her life story of being a pastor's wife or a missionary to faraway places. Does her "little" book have the same worth as that of a giant in the church world?

What about the book telling the story of a family devastated by mental illness or having a child die tragically or about having an adult son in prison for murder? What place do they have in the kingdom of God? What place do they have against a book like *Decision-Making and the Will of God?*

This was not at all an issue for Athena, but it was something I had to deal with. Were we advancing the kingdom or providing a service to satisfy the ego of some small-town preacher? I prayed.

The kingdom of God is made up of millions of stories, each impacting someone. Some of the stories are common to all of us—the struggle to survive, the struggle to serve God. But each is important, as it represents the working of God in an individual life. There are no small stories in God's kingdom. Each and every one is important and significant and should be told. Every story of God's goodness,

> There are no small stories in God's kingdom.

faithfulness, and glory needs to be shared.

Some stories are obviously not suitable for publication, that is true, and many interesting things happen to people who are unable to publish or have no desire to do so. But every story of "This is what God has done in my life" is worthy of telling.

Did we expect to take on such a righteous task without there being opposition? We didn't. But we were surprised from where the opposition came. It didn't come mostly from the

> Did we expect to take on such a righteous task without there being opposition?

outside but from people within the organization who had personal agendas that created tension in the ranks. The conflicts were personal rather than professional. There was little disagreement with what we wanted to accomplish, but personal wants and perceived needs had a propensity of bringing everything to a standstill.

Athena

The way God put me back into publishing with Redemption Press was breathtaking. At first, I took on the work because I felt I owed it to so many authors whom I'd abandoned by the closure of WinePress. Once the cult leader and his wife who took me for everything got the company out of my name, they cut me out of any meaningful work there. That left me with no voice and no authority. Many of these authors had signed with WinePress because they trusted me, so I felt responsible for the way many of them were mistreated by the people I'd allowed into management. I wanted to do whatever I could to make up for my error in judgment.

As a side note, if you're not familiar with my story of coming out of this horrendous decade plus of spiritual abuse, you might want to read my memoir that details how I found my way into deception and out again, fully redeemed and restored: *Full Circle: Coming Home to the Faithfulness of God*.

After starting Redemption Press, we spent the first few years just helping the orphaned WinePress authors get back into print or get their hands on their own files. Since I'd moved back into the former WinePress offices, I had access to all the digital files for the book covers, the manuscript files, the formatted interiors of the books, and even the e-book files. It felt like a miracle that we had everything there to give back to the authors what they had paid WinePress for. I wanted to do whatever I could to make amends, and that was the best way to start.

In 2016 and 2017, as Cross Books, Tate Publishing, and a few other publishers went out of business, I found myself helping other traumatized authors get their books back into print.

Once I had done everything I could to help the affected authors move on from very traumatic losses, I began to ask God what our own focus should be. The motto "Your Message—Our Mission" was our starting point, but I knew there was going to be more to it.

Before I would learn what God was leading me toward, I had more opposition to experience from within the camp.

> Before I could learn what God was leading me toward, I had more opposition to experience from within the camp.

In 2018 the Lord allowed Redemption Press to become a sponsor of the Women of Joy Tour where, by special invitation, we asked authors to join us in this opportunity to get their messages out to 50,000 women across the southern states. This included traveling to eight events in a year.

Before heading out, I'd hired some new team members to help navigate the surge of new authors that would certainly come from this promotion. Ross advised me to be more hands on with my staff and the hiring of new people. I didn't listen and paid dearly for it.

My avoidance of problems, hoping they would just resolve themselves, was not a viable leadership policy. I was definitely in the crucible of the furnace . . . the dross was rising to the surface, and it wasn't pretty.

While I was happily gallivanting all across the country with the Women of Joy Tour, the enemy had a field day at home as some employees took offense and division spread. After the tour wrapped up, an implosion happened at the home office. The office had become poisoned by toxic jealousy and bitterness, and some staff resigned. There were those who were jealous of others who went on road trips with me and couldn't understand why I didn't invite them to go. While my infrastructure was solidly in place for editing, design, typesetting, printing, and distribution, the administrative tasks handled by the home office were suddenly abandoned.

God had called me to build Redemption Press, but it had become a haven for the work of the enemy. My neglect in properly leading and shepherding my staff allowed the enemy to gain a foothold within. I had handed off leadership to those who were neither called nor equipped to do the job. I have to own this result because I was not the leader I needed to be. As a result, I had to spend months working six days a week for twelve hours a day. I knew I needed to get my hands on everything and every process to determine where we were.

> Work had to be surrounded by prayer in order to engage the warfare at hand.

Even years after the fact, I found out some of the authors who participated felt I was playing favorites on the Women of Joy Tour. More hurt feelings came into play, never to be resolved, only because they were never voiced to me.

I felt like Nehemiah who had to assess the state of the broken-down walls of Jerusalem and then take action to rebuild. This is where I learned the importance of being alert and sober minded, because the enemy was like a roaring lion just looking for someone to devour, and he'd found his target within the home office of Redemption Press.

I thought of how Nehemiah learned how to fight the naysayers who tried to destroy the work of God with intimidation, threats, and lies. Those committed to rebuild worked with one hand and held their weapons in the other. Work had to be surrounded by prayer in order to engage in the warfare at hand.

I learned during this time that allowing team members to stay offended or angry at some real or perceived wrongs meant they were going to bed angry. Ephesians 4:26–27 (ESV) tells us, "Be angry and do not sin; do not let the sun go down on your anger, and give no opportunity to the devil."

Ephesians 6:10–18 instructs us to put on the armor God gives us. I made a habit of intentionally doing this piece by piece every morning, out loud, to declare that Jesus is the victor.

Two more times in the next four years I would find myself in similar situations, with another group of those I failed to lead and shepherd who became offended and bitter. Still struggling with addressing conflict, I learned to pray, "Lord, if they are going to stay offended and let the enemy get a foothold, please move them on," and God answered that prayer every time.

Throughout all these challenges, I've been convicted that I've tried to relinquish my responsibility over and over to shepherd the team that God has given me—or allowed me to hire—to my own demise. I guess I'm a bit of a slow learner, but praise God, I'm making progress.

Amazingly, during this season of rebuilding in 2019, Redemption was chosen as the publisher for the high-profile companion devotional for the nationally-released *Unplanned* movie. Having my own experience with an unplanned pregnancy, and the abortion forced on me by my father when I was nineteen, I felt this was an incredible opportunity to watch God do his Romans 8:28 thing!

In the spring of 2019, God gave me clarity on his purpose for Redemption Press. As I pulled away in my Mini Cooper convertible from the conference center where I'd emceed the Northwest Christian Writer's Renewal, Mount Rainier was "out," the sun was shining, and all was right with the world. While I was still in a hard season of rebuilding, I felt some hope about the future.

Driving home surrounded by a jumble of books and display materials on that beautiful day, I mulled over the conference and the writers I had gathered with. Then the words "She Writes for Him" popped into my mind. Along with the words came an idea. What about creating a compilation book to give expression to women who had struggled with abuse, depression, and the fallout from abortion, betrayal, shame, and loss? This would help women in the church understand what others had gone through and how God had met them in it and restored them.

> With growing excitement, I asked, "Lord, is this from you?"

With a growing excitement, I asked, "Lord, is this from you?" The ideas kept unfolding as I continued driving south on I-5 toward our home in Enumclaw, and the concept felt so solid, so clear and right, that I felt God was in it.

I thought about how the compilations could include featured authors who were well known, along with first-time and newer authors. I knew this could help debut authors reach new audiences and provide a way for well-known authors to give back to those coming up the ranks. After my own years of spiritual abuse and being misunderstood by those in the church, I knew others with various issues were hurting from being shamed and shunned.

By the time I got home, the excitement was still building about the possibilities this could bring for so many. It would be whole new level of our message and mission! This was not just about publishing books but helping bring resolution to pain and showing readers they were not alone and were safe to express their own struggles.

> This was not just about publishing books but helping bring resolution to pain.

Less than a year later, a beautiful, award-winning, hardcover, full-color devotional journal *She Writes for Him: Stories of Resilient Faith* was a reality. And there was more . . . the She Writes for Him banner launched virtual conferences and training to help women across the nation connect with each other and find purpose during the isolation of the COVID-19 pandemic.

> What about organizing a virtual conference?

In March of 2020, one after another conference was canceled including all the places I was slated to teach on faculty. I thought, *What about organizing a virtual conference?*

By April 5, 2020, I had emailed author, editor, and industry professional friends and asked them to be a part of the first She Writes for Him virtual conference. By May 14, we had thirty-three faculty members headlining with Liz Curtis Higgs, Carol Kent, and Mary DeMuth. The online training saw 450 women gather for three days of inspiration, teaching on the craft of writing, and best of all, needed fellowship and relationship building. Many described the event as a cross between a women's retreat and writers conference without the stress of having to pitch agents and editors!

God knew the world would be in shutdown for large gatherings for the next two years, and he planted an idea that would bless and help many. He led us to pivot from in-person events to multiple types of virtual events. After that initial online conference, the She Writes for Him Bootcamp: 21 Days from Idea to Manuscript Blueprint was birthed, where more individualized help was given. Next came the ROAR Virtual Marketing Conference, followed by a She Writes for Him Write Your Hard Story 5-Day Challenge, to different themed virtual author reception tours. It was glorious to watch how God worked through these events to equip, encourage, and energize writers.

Our first Bootcamp was in session during May of 2020 when George Floyd was killed in Minneapolis and the marches and rioting were taking place in the streets of our cities across the nation. In our group of thirty women, there was one lone Black sister.

As we were wrapping up a session, someone turned to her and asked, "How are you doing?"

Her gracious answer opened up a conversation that left me heartbroken over the racial injustice commonplace in our country. I had no clue this kind of thing was happening to my Black sisters, and I was outraged.

That conversation led to a series of bonus *All Things* podcast interviews where I had conversations with many Black sisters in Christ to hear their stories of racial injustice and how God had brought good out of it in their lives. At the same time, we created a compilation to give our sisters a voice and help begin the conversation between Blacks and Whites within the church.

So far, *She Writes for Him: Black Voices of Women* has won two awards for second place in Inspirational/Gift Book of the Year at the Selah Awards and Golden Scroll Awards. I was also just honored with the 2022 Publisher of the Year Award from the Soul Café Awards for making a difference in the Pacific Northwest through creative arts.

My heart is filled with gratitude. I have been able to share truths I had gleaned on spiritual warfare during my long-ago time of ministry to veterans, with writers and speakers in keynotes I've given at the She Writes virtual events. I've shared how the tactics used by the Vietcong during the Vietnam War were completely opposite from the conventional warfare of previous wars. Guerrilla warfare is sneaky and camouflaged in the surroundings so you don't see the enemy, even though he is there. He may have buried explosives in the path ahead of you or even set trip wires to blow you up. Psychological warfare is used to demoralize the troops.

> Being a writer or storyteller in the kingdom of God brings with it spiritual warfare we must be ready for.

Isn't that the way the enemy of our souls works? Being a writer, storyteller, or worker in the kingdom of God brings with it spiritual warfare we must be ready for. If we don't understand the enemy's sneaky tactics, we can easily be side-lined, distracted, and discouraged by his constant harassment. "Who do you think you are to write a book?" or "No one wants to hear what you have to say!" or "If you tell your story, everyone will know the truth about you—that you're an impostor!"

I've also seen firsthand the importance of recognizing another aspect of the spiritual battle. Since Satan is the prince of the power of the air, one of his chief domains seems to be in technology. He uses it to lead people into captivity through the sin of online pornography and hinder relationships by capturing the minds and souls of children through their tablets and cell phones. I wonder if his specialty is the way he hinders technology when it is focused on glorifying God.

I'll never forget the time one of our team leaders came up against this wall. As our content creator and event manager for our Proclaim conference, Carol sent out a very important email to all the faculty who would be arriving the next day. She'd written the complicated and lengthy email late the night before within the email (not in a Word document saved on her computer).

When we got to work in the morning, Carol gasped. "It's gone. The email. Athena, it's nowhere to be found. And I don't have a copy of it! That means I need to spend the next two hours recreating the entire thing."

After scouring her MacBook, she came up empty and was extremely discouraged and frustrated. Already behind due to a bout of COVID that had taken her out for almost two weeks, she was buried in a to-do list that was way overdue.

After searching my inbox, then junk mail, and then everything on my laptop, I had just about resigned myself to the loss of the email. Then it hit me. *Wait a minute! No way Satan, you are not going to win this battle!*

I stood up and started to pray. "Lord, we really need your help. Would you please rebuke the devourer on our behalf? Would you dismantle every strategy of the evil one to hinder and block that email from getting to our faculty? Lord, I thank you that you are greater than he who is in the world . . . and I thank you in advance for whatever you will do to recover that email! In Jesus's name, amen!"

Less than sixty seconds later, we heard the "ding" as the email popped into all our inboxes.

Why had I waited so long before I prayed? It reminded me of all the other times I've hit roadblocks with technology—and that same prayer changed everything!

The same thing happened during the editing of this manuscript when parts of paragraphs randomly disappeared. This time, I quickly prayed aloud on the phone with our editor that God would rebuke the devourer in Jesus's name. After she restarted her computer, the missing pieces were back in place, and we had an important reminder that we always need to pray first.

As a result of watching God answer those types of warfare prayers, I've been able to teach our She Writes for Him attendees to equip themselves with the armor God gives us and resist the enemy—taking captive the lies he spews into our minds and replacing them with the truth of the Word of God. And take action when it seems there's pushback from the unholy realm.

Just recently, we held our third She Writes for Him 5-Day Challenge, centered around the "Write Your Hard Story" theme. Halfway through the challenge, I shared what the Lord had taught me back in my veteran's ministry days about our wounds becoming idols in our lives. I was in awe of how God used that truth as we encouraged over one hundred participants to make sure they were writing from their healed scars, not their wounds.

The last Write Your Hard Story session was over, and the leadership team was reviewing how the day had gone, when it hit me. All of a sudden, I felt overwhelmed by a sense of gratitude that God was accomplishing the vision that he'd given me three decades earlier. Here I was teaching women in the challenge how to understand the fallout of their own trauma and provide tools to help them move forward in their healing. All to prepare them to write their hard story. I could not hold back the tears as I shared my "aha" moment with the team.

> I felt overwhelmed by a sense of gratitude that God was accomplishing the vision he'd given me three decades earlier.

Many more "God moments" have taken place under the She Writes for Him banner that God has unfurled for us to minister under. I am in awe of the faithfulness of God.

And, amazingly, despite all the failures and blunders I've made as a leader, Redemption Press was named a "Best Christian Workplace" in late 2021 by the Best Workplace Institute.

This was one more encouragement from the Lord and a stellar "working all things for good" moment.

Discussion Questions
for Couples and Small Groups

1. God has put people in your life for a reason. Think about two or three that you know what their purpose was/is in your life. Put it in writing.
2. Can you give your testimony in a hundred words? Try it.
3. Someone is following you—where are you taking them?
4. It doesn't matter how many times you've traveled around the sun—as long as you have breath, God wants to use you. Are you willing?

CHAPTER 10

In All Things

Ross

There are few passages in the Bible that are more misused than Romans 8:28. Part of the confusion is caused, I think, by the different ways the translators have worded it. The *Revised Standard Version* and the *New King James Version* say, "all things work together for good." This is sometimes interpreted as everything that happens to a person is good and comes from God, which leads some people to the idea that every bad thing that ever happens to a person is God's fault, that we aren't responsible for the tragedies that befall us—it is what God wanted. This is not only a misreading of the text but also really bad theology.

The newer versions clarify the meaning, in my humble opinion. *The New Living Translation* says, "God causes everything to work together for the good." The *Contemporary English Version* says, "God is always at work for the good." These, I think, hit the real meaning of the text. The text doesn't make God responsible for the crazy, sinful, harmful, and devastating things that happen but says in them He works for our good, "for those that love God and are called to his purpose."

This a very significant difference.

There are things that happen to us just because we live in a fallen world, like cancer or diabetes. Other things happen to us because of really bad choices we make. The responsibility of such things is our own fault. But the good news is that whatever happens to us, whether because of our own sinfulness or because we live in a fallen world, God works for our good. That really is good news.

> There are things that happen to us just because we live in a fallen world.

I was a very precocious teenager. I had a girlfriend who was equally precocious. Which led to her getting pregnant. I was seventeen; she was eighteen. We married and stayed married for forty-nine years.

At the time, I figured God would withdraw the call I knew was on my life. I knew at an early age I was called to be a pastor. But how could that happen after committing such a sinful act, with such long-term consequences? Surely I had disqualified myself. Ah, but since I didn't actually want to be a pastor, maybe this wasn't as bad as it seemed.

And this was only the tip of the iceberg as far as my sins were concerned. I just couldn't see that God could ever use this pregnancy for anything that resembled good in my future.

> *Are you going to keep your word to me?*

When I was about twenty-six, I was happily driving along when I heard in my head, in my own voice, the words, *Are you going to keep your word to me?* It was so profound that I pulled over.

"What?" I said to myself. I am not the brightest guy, and I sure wasn't consistently in contact with God, but I knew who was talking to me. "What did you say?"

And I heard it in my head again. *Are you going to keep your word to me?* I knew instantly what he was talking about.

I thought, *Lord, I have a wife and two young sons. How can I go to Bible school? And who would want a jerk like me to be their pastor?*

This was all going on in my head as I sat by the side of Orange Grove Road in Tucson, Arizona. I had been raised in the church. I had been in Sunday school and attended summer vacation Bible school all my life. I had studied—been *forced* to study—the Bible all my childhood. I'd even memorized many verses.

> Can you understand why I believe so strongly in "irresistible grace"?

What popped into my head was *I can do all things through Christ who strengthens me.*

I don't think I remembered it was in Philippians 4:13, but the thought was there.

I said to God, "You still want me?"

And I heard, or thought, *Are you going to keep your word to me? You said you'd do whatever I wanted you to do. Are you going to keep your word?*

It would be hard for me to explain all that was going through my mind, but I knew I had to keep my word to God. And the amazing thing was that at that point I *wanted* to do it. Can you understand why I believe so strongly in "irresistible grace"? In an instant he had changed the trajectory of the rest of my entire life, and I was somehow happy about it.

"God causes everything to work together for the good of those who love God and are called to His purpose," says Romans 8:28 in the *New Living Translation. The Contemporary English Version* says, "God is always at work for the good." Always. You just have to love that. I knew I was called; I just didn't understand the profound truth of the entire passage.

I want to tell you that everything from that moment went smoothly and I became an amazing, righteous man. But, of course, you know that would be a lie. But Romans 8:28 became a staple in my theological life.

I don't remember how long Athena and I had been married before it became obvious that Romans 8:28 was equally important and profound to her. So much so that she named our bookstore Romans 8:28 Books.

In 2013, we discovered that my wife, Cathy, the girl I got pregnant in 1964, had cancer. We prayed, we anointed with oil, and we prayed some more. She stepped into Jesus's arms one hundred and twenty-six days later. As heartbroken as I was, I was not angry with God or bitter. I didn't even ask why. But I did question how he was going to make anything good come from this tragedy in my life.

Then came Athena. Not as a replacement—how does one replace the mother of your children and lover of forty-nine years? No, Athena wasn't a replacement; this was a new chapter in my life.

I've always been drawn to Isaiah 43:19 (NIV) where God tells the prophet, "See, I am doing a new thing! Now it springs up; do you not perceive it?"

A new thing. Did I see it? It was hard to miss. There have been several occasions in my life where God changed my direction or circumstances. So another change had sprung up. May his name be praised forever!

I don't much believe in coincidences, and God's participation in my life pretty much negates the effects of "accidents." No, Athena's entrance into my life was neither coincidence nor accident. Remember the thing about God's purposes? Yeah, me too.

So now what did God have in mind? "What purpose do you have in mind, Abba? What do you want us to do?"

Dr. R. C. Sproul, in his CD titled *Loved by God* (Ligonier Ministries), says,

> Romans 8:28 is one of the most comforting texts in all of Scripture. It assures the believer that all 'tragedies' are ultimately blessings. It does not declare that all things that happen are good in themselves but that in all the things that happen to us, God is working in and through them for our good. This is also firmly grounded in His eternal purpose for His people.[5]

Athena

I definitely have had to wrestle with the concept of God working good in *all things*. How could losing everything that mattered to me to a con man and his wife be turned to good?

After months of counseling, I began to see how much baggage I had from all my trauma as a child, teenager, and young mom. Then my son took me to an attorney to see if I could do anything about losing my company. He reviewed the paperwork from the so-called sale of WinePress Publishing.

As he turned the pages, he shook his head, growling out the words, "Fraud! Sham! What they did to you was criminal!"

As I sat there and took in what he was saying, it was as if a light bulb came on in my mind. What I'd experienced for those thirteen years in the cult was not God working at all but instead a sinister misuse of spiritual authority for personal power and financial gain. The sale of WinePress was a fraudulent transaction and a sham. I had been "had."

This husband-and-wife team—I had met the wife at a very credible writers conference—had used their position of authority as ministers of the gospel to ensnare me and my then husband, Chuck, into their web of deceit, manipulation, and control. They used Scriptures out of context to shame and shun us and led us to believe that we needed to be rescued from our "wide road" Christianity over to their "narrow road" truth.

As my husband pushed back on their demands for control, they fed me lies that he was probably cheating on me anyway, and "He doesn't really love God."

This started me on a road that led to them counseling me to divorce him (in Jesus's name, of course), cut my kids out of my life unless they agreed to the cult's doctrine, and any other family or friends who could not be won over. They even convinced me that I'd be in sin if I continued to try to run the business, since women had no place in authority over men.

I know, I know. It amazes me to look back and remember how badly I was deceived, but deceived I was.

But God! God was patiently, lovingly waiting to bring me back to life.

> The more God restored my understanding of his goodness and faithfulness, the more I began to be willing to own my part in where I'd ended up.

The more God restored my understanding of his goodness and faithfulness, the more I began to be willing to own my part in where I'd ended up. The biggest realization I encountered was the truth that my unhealed trauma had set me up to be vulnerable to deception.

In the years before I'd been ensnared by the couple, God had given me keen insight into the effects of post-traumatic stress disorder (PTSD) not only on Vietnam veterans but also on the women who married them. He opened my eyes to the spiritual fallout from these unhealed wounds and how they controlled us.

There are also physical and emotional responses to trauma, seen in the symptoms of PTSD, such as depression, anger, suicidal thoughts, isolation, difficulties with intimate relationships, and more.

When I looked in God's Word for the spiritual response to trauma so we could see healing be complete, I was astonished to find this answer. Psalm 147:3 (ESV) says, "He heals the broken hearted and binds up their wounds." The Hebrew root word for wound from this passage is *atstebeth*. The *Hebrew-Greek Key Word Study Bible* defines atstebeth as "it is an idol."

When I read this, it made immediate sense to me. If the wound is not healed, it is constantly being triggered. When we are triggered, we respond to that stimuli with ungodly reactions. Fight or flight . . . anger or depression, and oh, so much more.

Years earlier as I learned this, I began to teach others about wounds without ever allowing God to heal my own wounds. "Do as I say, not as I do" was the order of the day. I had not repented for allowing my own wounds to become my idols. Sure, I acknowledged the sin, but I did not take action to move toward God's healing for those infected places in my soul, so the repentance was not complete. Consequently, the wounds festered, providing an opening for the enemy to bring deception into my life. Heartbreak and unbelievable destruction in my relationships and my family's life resulted.

Could God ever bring anything good out of that rebellion and disobedience?

The more I grew in grace and finally allowed God to heal me, the more he began to restore what the enemy had stolen. Romans 8:28 became real to me as I stopped considering myself a victim and instead owned my own sin that had led to my deception. And I was set free.

There is so much God has done to use my newfound freedom from that horrible deception in my life to speak hope to others. He has shown his faithfulness and his goodness and worked all things together for my good.

Discussion Questions
for Couples and Small Groups

1. In all things God works for the good of those who love Him and are called according to His purpose. Do you believe it? Do you have an example?
2. Is there a new thing God wants to do in your life? Can you name it?
3. Is there some healing that has to take place before you might venture out again?

CHAPTER 11

Perils and Pleasures
of Serving God

Ross

There have been many things I've enjoyed about being in vocational ministry and some things I've not enjoyed so much. At one point in my life, I was district chairman for the Pacific Northwest District of the Evangelical Free Church of America. I didn't do so well; I'm not much into meetings and rules of order, but I did enjoy having close contact with other pastors in our district. As one who has been a pastor for a prolonged period of time, I was often asked about how certain things were done or how certain people were dealt with. I always like sharing with others what God has taught me in ministry.

For those who have never discussed with their pastor what professional ministry is like, let me say, it is messy. While it is true that, as a pastor, I've been invited to share some of the joys and celebrations in congregants' lives, most often pastors get called when people are in some kind of trouble or pain. No one ever called me in the middle of the night to tell me how happy they were or how gracious God is.

No, when my phone rings at two in the morning it is because somebody is in crisis; somebody needs bail money, somebody is in the hospital, or somebody just died. That's what I get in the middle of night. And that is all right; it's as it should be—when in trouble or need, call me.

But it is never convenient. It's never easy to rise in the early hours, dress, and venture out to some catastrophe. Often when someone tells me they think they are called to the pastorate, I say, "Run, run, run away." If one is truly called to it, he or she will not be able to run away.

If one is called, being a pastor is a great job. It is rewarding and satisfying, in spite of the inconvenience and difficulty of doing the job well. If one is not actually called by God, it is a hard and pitiful existence. I've known both cases. I've known people who took to it and served for decades. And I've known those who were in over their heads almost immediately and left bitter and angry. I've tried to minister to both.

There is an old axiom, which I've found to be frightfully true, that says, "Most pastors quit on Mondays." I've had many, many Mondays when I've had enough; I was finished and wanted to resign. I've never really done it, but there is something about Mondays.

In the sixties, a group called The Mamas and the Papas sang a song called "Monday, Monday." I think they must have heard the lamentations of some cleric somewhere. On lots of Mondays, lamenting was my theme.

Mondays always come after Sundays. After speaking the words God has given us, I know most of the folks who nod and say amen will forget all that was said before they get to the parking lot. Or, after I've spoken, there is the goodhearted soul who feels he needs to tell me how wrong I was and proceeds to correct something that I'd spent hours and hours studying and preparing.

So Monday mornings I may wake up thinking there must be a better job out there somewhere. But Tuesday finds me again in the study reading the next passage of Scripture in the series and putting together a title and outline.

Then some young preacher calls and says, "Let's have coffee. I need to talk to you." One experienced in such calls knows by the tone of the caller's voice what is coming.

The next day or so finds us in some coffee shop having a heart-to-heart. Many times I've heard, "I don't think I can go on in this role." Sometimes, after hearing their tale of woe, I agree; it's time to go. Their work is done at whatever church they are serving. It happens. But most often I've found this poor soul just needs to be reminded why he is in this vocation, why he went to seminary, and why he accepted a call to the First Church of the Whatever in the first place.

> Most often, after this person hears himself talk, and sometimes after hearing me talk, he realizes he just needed to vent.

Most often, after this person hears himself talk, and sometimes after hearing me talk, he realizes he just needed to vent. He needed to talk to someone who knows the perils of being a pastor.

It may be hard to believe, but I've always enjoyed those conversations. I think I said earlier that one of my spiritual gifts is encouragement. These conversations are prime examples of opportunities to put my gifting into practice.

Now, because of my advancing years, I'm moving toward less involvement in the church I pastor. And that's where my relationship with Athena comes into play. As a partner in Redemption Press, I get to work with people who are telling their stories in written form.

With so many years in publishing, she has a long track record of doing this. But it is new to me. However, after years of writing sermons and articles, and after years of coaching younger pastors, I find I have some talent for it. And, because of my encouragement gift, it seems to be natural. To date, I've only had limited exposure to the publishing world, but it is easy to see, since I'm half owner of a publishing house, I anticipate great opportunities.

Writing Christian books is a ministry. I guess that goes without saying, but many I've chatted with have not thought of it as such. Most of the books we publish are people telling their stories of life. And, since we publish Christian books, they are about what God has done, or is doing, in the author's life.

As I mentioned, we take our motto "Your Message—Our Mission" very seriously. And we want to do it the very best we can. We hire the best editors, coaches, illustrators, and formatters that we can find. We believe that God calls us to excellence, both as authors and publishers. Our goal is to take an author's blood, sweat, and tears and put them into a product that will please God, meet a felt need in readers, benefit his kingdom, and make the author happy. Not always an easy task.

Athena

I've realized that one of the components of serving God in equipping and empowering those with a story of redemption is protecting the gospel. After my detour into deception, this is super important to me.

In today's publishing space, anyone can write anything and be an author on Amazon. No one is going to stop you and say, "Umm, this is not ready," or "This is not an accurate use of biblical text," or "The quotes you are using are out of bounds for fair use copyright laws."

Anyone can write a book and skip coaching, developmental editing, line editing, copyediting, and proofreading. They can just upload a document and instantly become published.

But will the work have credibility? Hardly.

> Coming out of a New Age background, I am especially sensitive to the movements in the church today that embrace New Age practices.

Will they handle God's Word with accuracy and integrity or find their theology on Google (which may mean it's out of context)? This is one reason why, at Redemption, we've partnered with Logos Bible Software to offer resources to equip our authors with all they need to rightly divide the Word of God.

Coming out of a New Age background, I am especially sensitive to the movements in the church today that embrace New Age practices. I've even heard Christians proclaim that the New Age belongs to God and we need to take those practices back and sanctify them.

Because of my background, I can confidently tell you this is not a biblical perspective. For example, some Christians have been lured into the belief that our words have power and can manifest what we want in our lives. It is true that our words can tear down or build up, but only the Word of God has the power to change a heart and bring repentance, redemption, and restoration. For us to think we can decree and declare something we are not promised by God is to follow the enemy into a trap.

To decree and declare that "I can do all things through Christ who strengthens me" (Phil. 4:13 NKJV) is only partially correct. This verse was written by the apostle Paul from prison declaring he had learned the secret of being content in lack and in plenty and that he can do all things, even face need and hunger, through Christ who gives him strength.

> It is true that our words can tear down or build up, but only the Word of God has the power to change a heart and bring repentance, redemption, and restoration.

The truth of this Scripture is that no matter what God allows in our lives, whether it's a storm or smooth sailing, he will give us the strength to walk through it. It is not that we can do *anything*, like lift 300 pounds or win a gold medal in the Olympics or learn a foreign language overnight or become a *New York Times* bestselling author!

No wonder so many are deconstructing their faith when they have been given false hope by Scriptures taken out of context. This makes me so sad.

If I decree and declare, "I am highly favored by God," but am in disobedience; harbor unforgiveness; verbally, emotionally, or physically abuse my spouse; or commit some other sin without repenting, that is a lie. Saying it out loud will not change the truth.

We are to humbly come to our God in supplication, not demanding an answer. We are told to "boldly draw near to the throne of grace" (Heb. 4:16), as he hears us and knows our needs.

Verses are often taken out of context by those who follow the demand and decree practices. This can easily result in presumption. The Scripture should instead give us greater insight into our part in the process of petition.

The end of Romans 4:17 (NKJV) says, "Who ... calls those things which do not exist as though they did". And yet the context tells us it is not about *us* calling things which do not exist as though they do, but this refers to God. *He* is the one who calls things which do not exist into existence! This verse helps us recognize the characteristics of God who can do all things, not what man can do.

Abraham recognized that the promises of God would be accomplished, but he had to trust—specifically that he would have a son in his old age (see Romans 4:16–17).

> If I decree and declare, "I am highly favored by God," but am in disobedience; harbor unforgiveness; verbally, emotionally, or physically abuse my spouse; or commit some other sin without repenting, that is a lie.

What are you asking God for today? In humility, first discover God's promises in his Word that meet every need of your life and trust Him. Then you can declare those things that are true to His character ...

"God, you are holy."

"God, you are just."

"God, you are righteous."

These are declarations that will set you on a path of complete trust in God's character so you can rest in his promises.

Now that's a practice that is sanctified!

I find more and more that I long to understand Scripture in context. Ross and I talk about whether a certain Scripture is a promise for us or if it was just for the people at that time in history. I ask him if a verse really means what it sounds like, or does it mean something else?

As we discuss the Word and allow iron to sharpen iron, as the verse goes, we grow to love God and one another even more.

Discussion Questions
for Couples and Small Groups

1. Are you serving God, or are you an observer of others' ministries? Are you content with how you serve Him? Is He?
2. What changes have to be made to get back in the game? Are you willing to make them?
3. Have you ever heard a Scripture quoted out of context? How did you respond to it?

CHAPTER 12

Passing the Baton

Ross

Some years ago, there was much said and written about how older leaders in the church should "pass the baton" to younger leaders. Books were written about how to do it. And, I suppose, there were many who gladly passed on their responsibilities and faded into the sunset. In 2018, my friend Dr. Chuck Stecker wrote a book called *If You've Passed the Baton, Take It Back.*[6] His point was that the church needs its older, hopefully wiser, members to stay in the battle.

Chuck wrote this describing his book. It also explains what I'm addressing.

> Passing the baton refers to when one runner in a relay race passes the baton to the next runner. What is rarely considered when the runner completes the passing of the baton is that he or she must quit running, step off the track, and stay out of the race. In summary, the person is finished! In the United States, we have two generations of seniors who feel they have been told their time is over. They have been told to pass the baton, quit running, and get off the track—they are no longer needed in the race.

We must have a shift in our thinking. We have confused the baton of engagement with the mantle of leadership. As seniors, we must embrace the concept of pouring into the next generation, passing the mantle of leadership, and staying in the race until God calls us home.

I started pastoring when I was twenty-six years old. I had energy, endurance, and drive. For a while, I was bi-vocational. That was okay. I could do seventy-hour weeks standing on my head. I hadn't yet been to Bible school or seminary, but I'd been watching preachers—good preachers—for twenty-six years. I had a basic understanding of what worked and what didn't. I had a small library of commentaries and journals. I was all set. But what I didn't have was much life experience. And that's the part I want to talk about.

What Dr. Stecker says about passing the baton and quitting the race strikes at my heart. In my early years, I pastored a small church that had an abundance of older—*seasoned*, I like to say—people. These people, especially the women, had been the Sunday school teachers, the choir members, the janitors, and the nursery workers for years. But, by the time I got there, most of them had stepped down to let younger people, again mostly women, take over their jobs.

I understand the "seasoned" people aren't as energetic or quick as they were years ago, but here was a wealth of wisdom, experience, and talent sitting on the sidelines, or on the pew, just watching.

> "What are we gonna do when you retire or if something happens to you?"

What a shame.

I am in a transition in my life. A few years ago, our elders started talking about us needing a succession plan. Their question was, "What are we gonna do when you retire or if something happens to you?" I understood their concerns, though I wondered if they were just wanting to get rid of me, as I was in my mid-sixties then.

As it happened, there was a young man pastoring a very small Foursquare Church in town. He and I had struck up a friendship and often had conversations about life and the church.

One day I felt inspired to ask him, "What would you think about us merging our two churches together?" It came out absolutely spontaneously. I hadn't consciously given it much thought. It just sort of popped out of my mouth.

It took nearly ten years, but this year we finally merged New Life Foursquare Church with The Summit, the church I planted and have pastored for thirty-six years. It is too long a story to tell you here, but just let me say it has been good. But it hasn't been as easy as I thought it would be.

My thoughts early on were that we'd copastor for a few years and then I'd step back and be a teaching pastor or pastor emeritus or some such thing. When the dust settled after months of negotiation, it was decided that we'd serve as copastors for six months or so, I'd take a sabbatical, and Marcus would take over as lead pastor. That was what everybody, except me, wanted. Still believing this merger was of God, I had no option but to go along.

That is the hard part. As I'm writing today, the six months are coming to the end. I'm not ready to retire, emotionally, spiritually, or financially. I know there are some in the congregation who would like me to retire and go away. I am old, you know, but I'm not ready to retire and go away. I have years and years and years of experiences stored up—some good, some not so good, some of God, some driven by my ego. I've learned some things that only years in the saddle provide. And there

> My almost constant prayer is, "Lord, what do you want me to do now?"

might even be some hard-won wisdom within the clutter.

What do I do with all this? I agree it's time to change, but change comes hard, especially at seventy-five.

My almost constant prayer is, "Lord, what do you want me to do now?" Actually, that's been my prayer off and on for years, but it has real significance now in this time of transition. What's next? I have to pass the mantle of being the senior pastor—that's a given. But, using the racing metaphor, maybe I'm leaving one race for another, but I'm still running. Does that make sense?

I have always believed and taught that in seeking the will of God, one prays and looks for open doors. That isn't original

> I have always believed and taught that in seeking the will of God, one prays and looks for open doors.

with me, obviously; that's been taught by many of the giants of the church past. Many, including the new pastor, have expressed their desire to see me stay and minister in the new church, Plateau Community Church. So that is still an open door.

Then there is Redemption Press. Athena has wanted me to be more involved in that from its inception. Another open door. This transition is a bit scary but also exciting. I've been released from my responsibility of being lead pastor, but I have not been released from serving my Lord.

The apostle Paul knew his time had come to an end. He knew his race was about over. He wrote, "I have fought the good fight, I have finished the race, I have kept the faith" (2 Tim. 4:7 ESV).

I'm not there yet, at least as far as I know. I don't believe it's time to throw in the towel.

David told his son Solomon not to quit until the work was done. He said, "Be strong and courageous and do it. Do not be afraid and do not be dismayed, for the Lord God, even my God, is with you. He will not leave you or forsake you, until all the work for the service of the house of the Lord is finished" (1 Chron. 28:20 ESV).

If you are a seasoned Christian, what does the future hold for you? Are you at the end, are you still in the race, or have you passed the baton and quit the race?

Athena

As I approach my seventieth year, I ask God how he wants to use us together in a new way.

When Ross mentioned how he feels the most alive when he is teaching or preaching from the pulpit, I wondered if the three-month sabbatical coming up wasn't an opportunity for us to travel and speak as a couple, meet with friends and authors across the country, and continue to build up the kingdom of God as we go.

We've learned some things together and have been surprised at how God has worked and has allowed us to glory in His faithfulness.

Have you seen God's faithfulness in your life and in your walk with him? Then you have a story to tell. Do you realize your story can bring someone else some hope? It may not ever be written in a book, but you may share it just sitting down for dinner or coffee and talking about how God has brought good out of the struggles of your life.

Perhaps your words will restore faith in someone who's experienced church hurt or trauma that's still raw. Perhaps your journey of growing in grace through the struggles, rather than turning away in bitterness, will speak to someone on the brink of giving up on God. You never know what words God might use to begin a spark of restoration in one who feels dry and distant.

> Have you seen God's faithfulness in your life and in your walk with him? Then you have a story to tell.

Your story matters, no matter how it's shared. Our purpose is to glorify God in our journey so others can trust him for themselves.

Ross and I have told our own stories together to encourage you that God will be faithful to you in your relationships, no matter what age or stage you find yourself in. We hope our sharing helps you seek and find purpose in your own life. Most of all, we hope you'll never forget how God is faithful to bring good *in all things* for those called according to his purpose.

Enjoy the journey—as through the *all things* he works for good in our lives he continues to conform us to his image!

Discussion Questions
for Couples and Small Groups

1. If you are older, is there a theme to what God has done with you?
2. List three major things that God has taught you that younger people need to know. Are you willing to tell them?
3. Is your life in transition? How are you dealing with it?
4. Are you still in the race, or have you "passed the baton"? If you're still in the race, how would someone know?

How Can We Help?

We stand ready to help you bring your own story to life, publish through Redemption Press, or train and learn through the She Writes for Him Conferences and retreats. We are also ready to speak to your group, church, marriage, or seniors ministry!

Contact us at: www.redemption-press.com to discuss how we can assist you.

Notes

1. Margaret Atwood, *Moral Disorder and Other Stories* (Toronto, Canada: McClelland and Stewart Ltd.), 2006.

2. Patrick Rothfuss, *The Name of the Wind* (New York City: DAW Books), 2007.

3. Salman Rushdie, Salman Rushdie Quotes, BrainyQuote. com, BrainyMedia Inc, 2022, https://www.brainyquote.com/ quotes/salman_rushdie_140560.

4. Dr. Kevin Leman, *The Birth Order Book: Why You Are the Way You Are* (Grand Rapids, MI: Revel, 1985, 1998, 2009).

5. Dr. R. C. Sproul, CD, *Loved by God* (Ligonier Ministries).

6. Chuck Stecker, *If You've Passed the Baton, Take It Back* (Littleton, CO: Seismic Publishing Group), 2018.